GLYNDEBOURNE

A VISUAL HISTORY

GLYNDE

BOURNE

A VISUAL HISTORY

EDITED BY
BRIGITTE LARDINOIS
AND VAL WILLIAMS

WITH TEXT BY
SIR GEORGE CHRISTIE

CONTENTS

FOREWORD

There was unanimous approval of the idea of a celebratory photographic book to commemorate our 75th anniversary, as we have a truly spectacular archive spanning our 75 years, with many celebrated and dedicated photographers recording our unique and colourful history. One of our guiding principles has always been to engage artists who are at the beginning of their careers and it is fascinating to see photographs of many of these personalities in their early stages. It was not hard to choose a narrator and I am not sure that my father knew what he was committing himself to when I casually asked him if he would write a few words for our anniversary book – what comes through are his very personal reminiscences of Glyndebourne through the ages.

Credit for researching the archive and selecting all the photographs goes to Brigitte Lardinois and Val Williams, and also to Joanna Townsend and Julia Aries – if they had had their way, the book would have been double the size – so apologies to those who have contributed to Glyndebourne throughout our history and who did not make the final cut. Most of the images were selected on their artistic merit and so this book is as much a celebration of photography as an art form as it is a celebration of our history. Looking back at the 1930s compared to now, it feels as if the essence of Glyndebourne has not changed and we are still aiming to achieve the same artistic excellence now as we did then.

Gus Christie
Executive Chairman

INTRODUCTION

I make no apology in this chronological pictorial history of Glyndebourne for concentrating largely on the Festival, which, after all, is the engine room of Glyndebourne's output. But this should not detract from the importance we attach to the contribution of our Touring Company and education department to the canvas of varied creative activity that represents Glyndebourne's contribution to opera in this country. I have also ignored our quite extensive tours abroad to places as disparate as Hong Kong, New York and the length and breadth of Europe.

I have shamelessly name-dropped in my account to provide narrative colour to the pictorial story – and in the process have omitted a multitude of artists who merit mention. I apologise for this but there simply wasn't room.

George Christie

The production of *Glyndebourne – A Visual History*
is sponsored by Gerald Hyam and Siemens plc

SIEMENS

1930s

The birth and early development of Glyndebourne have been recounted many times – more or less truthfully and, more often than not, romantically. The risk of repetitious banality makes my hand tremble in writing this opening chapter.

My father, born in December 1882, chose to pursue physics as the subject on which to base his career. However, in his 40s he developed a keen interest in and love for music – which resulted in the building of the Organ Room as a grandiose statement and adjunct to the home he had inherited and substantially altered. The house had been a fine example of Victorian architecture (Mark Girouard, in his majestic book on Victorian buildings, *The Victorian Country House*, gives Glyndebourne one line in his appendices: '*Glyndebourne: a house of which Mozart would have been ashamed.*').

It was in the Organ Room that my father mounted 'pro-am' performances of opera which in 1930 brought him together with my mother, a professional singer, Audrey Mildmay. Six months later they married – and four years thereafter Glyndebourne was born, conceived from their passion for opera and from, thankfully, the depth of his pocket.

The theatre seated a mere 330 with good acoustics, a stage with, in particular, a superb lighting system made by Siemens (my father's personal choice – and pride and joy) and a pass-door between stage and front-of-house which could accommodate only thin singers ...

The greatest stroke of good fortune for my parents was Fritz Busch's and Carl Ebert's acceptance to conduct and direct Glyndebourne's opening productions of *Figaro* and *Così* in 1934 – and to become Glyndebourne's Music Director and Artistic Director respectively. Busch and Ebert were refugees

1930
Audrey Mildmay sang at an

1931
Marriage of John Christie and

1932

1933
Birth of Rosamond Agnes

1934
First Glyndebourne Festival

from Nazi Germany. They were not Jewish, but held a deep repugnance for Hitler's emerging regime.

The appointment of these two eminent artists led inevitably to contact with – and ultimately contracts with – many of the great international singers of the day. In turn it led, too, to the appointment in 1936 of Rudolf Bing, possibly – even probably – the best impresario of his day. While Ebert and Busch brought artistic stature to Glyndebourne, Bing brought professionalism 'in spades' to the administration and presentation of their work. This, combined with my parents' passion, sense of direction and determination, created a chemical amalgam which exploded on pre-war England – and in the downlands of Sussex.

My father's exploits in the rural byways of Sussex were considered to be potty, but the first Festival in 1934 was generally acclaimed a success which, though showing no financial return on his investment, urged him and my mother to lay longer-term plans for the Festival.

Mozart's operas continued to be the seasonal diet until 1938 when Verdi's *Macbeth* (the first professional production in England of the revised 1865 version) and Donizetti's *Don Pasquale* were added to the programme.

It is odd now – some 75 years later when there is virtually no further capacity for contriving new interpretations in the production of Mozart's operas – to think that these works were not mainstream at the time. Glyndebourne's greatest pre-war contribution to the operatic repertoire was to equate the dramatic content with the musical content of the works, effectively bringing them theatrically alive. Directors in opera companies were frequently of secondary importance, to the extent that they were given no credit in programmes. Ebert with Busch brought a new dimension to the Mozart canon.

Outside Germany, singers ruled the world of operatic performance in the 18th and 19th centuries. Conductors then ruled from the 1920s until directors held sway from the 1950s to the present day.

By 1936 my father had invested substantial additional money into a large dressing-room block and a second restaurant, which were lacking in the first two seasons. His single-minded determination (and the depth of his pocket) – together with his selection of the artistic team – was what set the seal on Glyndebourne's early growth.

But he was not just an idealist. To get where he got before the war inevitably meant he had to be and was a realist. He was from the start financially independent and very soon the company was commercially self-sufficient in the sense that Glyndebourne made all its own costumes, props, wigs and (by virtue of ownership of a local building company) scenery – something which you won't find in today's 'country house opera' companies ... He even went so far as to run the restaurants – and stock the wine in a cellar which he built and sealed against water in his covered reservoir at the end of the back drive, so providing an almost totally consistent temperature for the wine.

King George VI invited my father to be his Kellermann at Buckingham Palace because of his extensive knowledge of, in particular, German wines, but he declined on the grounds that he had enough on his plate to get on with.

My mother was invited to sing Susanna in *Le nozze di Figaro* at Salzburg following the Glyndebourne Festival in 1939, but this was embargoed by the Foreign Office because of the heightening tension with Germany. The ensuing war changed the course of my mother's career and Glyndebourne's development – a change which resulted in ...

1935

1936

Official appointment of Rudolf Bing as General Manager

1937

1938

First full-length radio broadcasts from Glyndebourne

First professional production of *Macbeth* in the UK

1939

Audrey's invitation to sing Susanna at Salzburg Festival embargoed

Outbreak of the Second World War

ILSE BING
1937

An unchanging view of the lake lawns, 1937 (ILSE BING)

ABOVE: Looking through the yew hedges and Rose Garden (now called the Urn Garden) to the lawns beyond (BILL BRANDT)

LEFT: An early view of the house, the Organ Room and back wall of the original opera house seen from the Wild Garden, 1934 (A CONSOLE)

BELOW: The dressing-room and green-room block added in 1935 was built within an existing row of Irish yews. John Christie hated cutting down trees and always tried to work around them

ABOVE: The opera house, 1936, seen from the walled kitchen garden in which it was built. Initially incorporating merely an existing lily pond and a couple of flower borders, the Walled Garden, as it became known, was established in 1937 (BILL BRANDT)

BELOW: In 1938 the fly tower was added to allow the flying of scenery as opposed to pulling it out onto the grass at the side of the theatre. In this picture, one of the two contracted gardeners mows the lawn (a job now done using a ride-on mower)

OPPOSITE: Mr Harvey (Head Gardener) watering the newly created flower garden in what had been the walled kitchen garden. Mr Harvey landscaped the gardens in the early 1930s and developed and maintained them until 1959/60. He used a combination of formality (yew hedges) and informality (open spaces with vistas of the Downs). An indomitable character, Mr Harvey prevented Edmund Warre (Glyndebourne's architect) from putting up a summerhouse where he had just opened up a view of the Downs, and would happily leave a clump of buttercups in the borders

ABOVE: Local seamstresses making costumes for the first productions in one of the rooms in Glyndebourne house, 1934 (A CONSOLE)

OPPOSITE TOP: The wardrobe department in the dressing-room block, 1938

OPPOSITE BOTTOM: Costume fitting for chorus ladies in *Macbeth*, 1938

LEFT AND OPPOSITE BOTTOM:
Making, moving and painting scenery – outside and in the emptied restaurant, 1936. In 1924 John Christie took over the lease of the Royal Opera House at Tunbridge Wells. He ran it for a relatively short time, but in the process he learned a great deal about the running of a theatre, as well as finding there the indispensable Jock Gough, Glyndebourne's first Stage Foreman (BILL BRANDT)

LEFT: George Curry (Props Master), Jock Gough (Stage Foreman), Rudolf Bing (Manager), and designer Hamish Wilson (BILL BRANDT)

ABOVE: A member of John Christie's staff inspecting the lighting rig with Tuppy the pug dog. John Christie always insisted that the dogs were really in control

OPPOSITE: Mr EL Andrews and Props Master George Curry working on the props for *Macbeth*, 1938

No. 18
6 OZ.

TOP: Company members arriving by bus from Lewes Station, 1936 (BILL BRANDT)

ABOVE: The Chorus rehearsing in the Organ Room, 1938

OPPOSITE: Dancers rehearsing outside on the lawn

TOP: Roy Henderson, who sang at Glyndebourne between 1934 and 1940, posing in costume as Papageno for an informal snapshot. He went on to become an influential singing teacher

LEFT: The Three Boys in costume outside the Organ Room: Winifred Radford, Jean Beckwith and Mollie Mitchell

RIGHT: On-stage rehearsal for *Die Zauberflöte*, 1936: Carl Ebert, Mollie Mitchell, Aulikki Rautawaara, Jean Beckwith, Winifred Radford, Hans Oppenheim and Rudolf Bing, with Fritz Busch in the pit

ABOVE: Carl Ebert (right) working with John Brownlee and Winifred Radford during a rehearsal of *Don Giovanni*, 1936 (BILL BRANDT)

OPPOSITE TOP: Fritz Busch conducting an orchestral rehearsal for *Macbeth* with the principals, including Margherita Grandi and Francesco Valentino, in the Christie Dining Hall, 1938

OPPOSITE BOTTOM: John Christie sitting on the counter of the Christie Dining Hall during an orchestral rehearsal, 1939 (FELIX MAN)

ABOVE: Salvatore Baccaloni as Bartolo, *Le nozze di Figaro*, in his dressing room
BELOW: Rehearsal for *Macbeth* on stage, 1938. The spear carriers were drawn from the ranks of the restaurant waiters, and the tallest boys from Lewes Grammar School
OPPOSITE: *Macbeth* dancers backstage, 1938

Le nozze di Figaro

ABOVE: Roy Henderson as the Count and Audrey Mildmay as Susanna, 1934 (CECIL KERR)

OPPOSITE: Aulikki Rautawaara as the Countess and John Brownlee as the Count, 1937 (ILSE BING)

ILSE

ABOVE: Entrance of the Commendatore's statue in *Don Giovanni*, with Salvatore Baccaloni as Leporello, David Franklin as the Commendatore and John Brownlee as Don Giovanni, 1936 (BILL BRANDT)
BELOW: *Don Pasquale*, with Salvatore Baccaloni in the title role and Mariano Stabile as Malatesta, 1938
OPPOSITE: Fiordiligi and Dorabella, *Così fan tutte*, 1937 (ILSE BING)

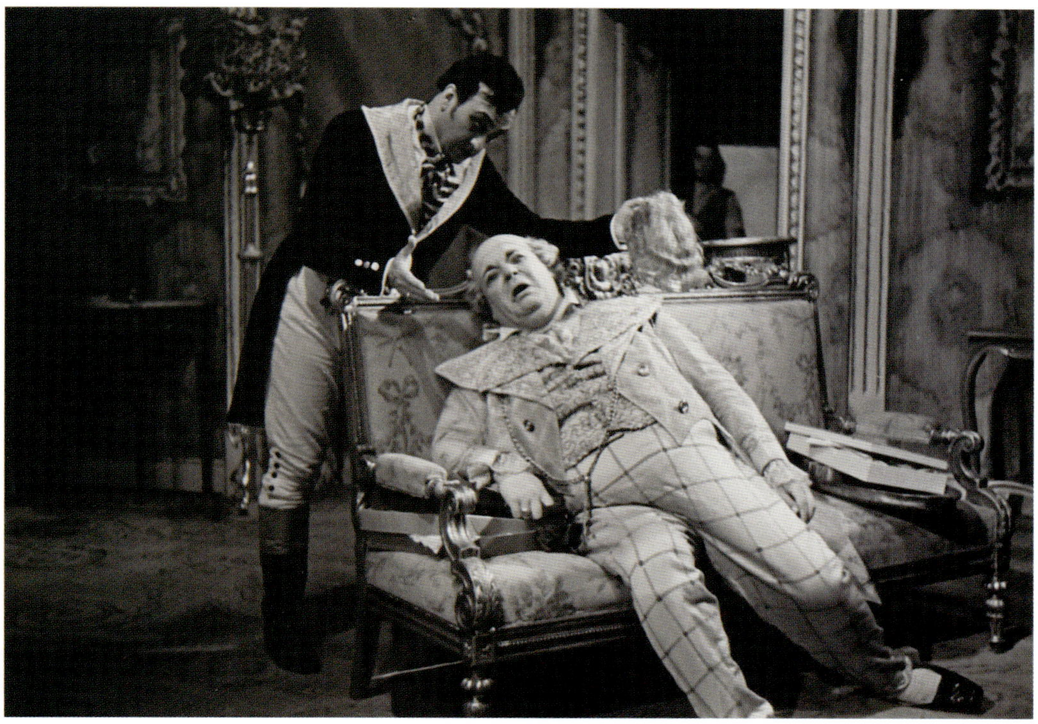

The Christies:
Audrey, George, Rosamond and John, 1937 (BASSANO)

Pages from Jani Strasser's photograph album, with his handwritten captions, 1934

Members of the Orchestra.
Aulikki Rautawaara
Rehearsal for Concert
in „Entführung" set

EAGLE
INSURANCE CO
14
PULLMAN CAR ON THIS TRAIN
SUPPLEMENTARY FARES
FIRST CLASS 2/- THIRD CLASS 1/-
HAIRDRESSING
SALOON
EASTBOURNE. (FRONT)
BEXHILL, HASTINGS & ORE. (REAR)
ZOO
BRIGHTON BELLE
PULLMAN CARS (ONLY)
SEAT TICKETS CAN BE OBTAINED AT BOOKING OFFICE.
BRIGHTON (NON STOP)
MITCHAM JUNCTION, SUTTON
CHEAM, EPSOM

ABOVE: The front drive in use as a chauffeurs' car park, 1936 (BILL BRANDT)

OPPOSITE: Members of the audience at Victoria Station, 1939. After five Glyndebourne seasons, the sight of people in evening dress in the afternoon did not cause too much of a stir

CHAUFFEUR'S
BAR

ABOVE: Audience members during dinner in the long interval in the first restaurant, the Christie Dining Hall, 1934

OPPOSITE: In 1935 the Chauffeurs' Bar was added to the back of the Mildmay Dining Hall kitchens

THE NEXT ACT
BEGINS AT
6-45
BROADCASTING

ABOVE: A rare group picnicking in the field. Picnicking only started to become popular after the war

OPPOSITE: The summer was cold in 1936 – two well-wrapped opera-goers in the Rose Garden (BILL BRANDT)

THE NEXT ACT
BEGINS AT
8.15

567562.

ABOVE: Long shadows on the Green Room lawn, 1936 (BILL BRANDT)

OPPOSITE: Audience members on the ha-ha lawn, 1938

1940s

... closure of the theatre, but not quite the discontinuation of the company's operation. A production of John Gay's *The Beggar's Opera* was mounted in 1940 to tour the regions, with John Gielgud directing, and featuring Michael Redgrave as Macheath and my mother as Polly Peachum – landing up, in May of that year, after six weeks, in the Haymarket Theatre in London.

By this time, the war had hotted up causing any plans or dreams for Glyndebourne's continued operation to be disbanded. The house, theatre, its buildings and the grounds at Glyndebourne were given over to and over-run by evacuee children from the East End of London for the duration of the war – a total transformation of the use of the premises.

Come the end of the war, various ideas were discussed and plans laid with Beecham (Sir Thomas Beecham) to revive the Festival, all of which came to virtually nought. Instead a partnership was formed with Benjamin Britten resulting in the first performances of his *Rape of Lucretia* with Kathleen Ferrier and Peter Pears (who had been in the Chorus before the war). This was the only opera performed at Glyndebourne in its 1946 resurrection after the war. *The Rape* then went out on an extensive tour, financially underwritten by my father. At the end of this tour, my father, so the story goes, was presented with a bill by Britten amounting to twice the agreed sum. A row ensued but, according to my understanding, due to a commitment to a continuing collaboration between Britten and Glyndebourne the following year, my father coughed up – rancorously.

Between 1946 and 1947 Britten formed the English Opera Group which then staged a reprise of *The Rape* and mounted the world premiere of *Albert Herring*, directed by Frederick Ashton with Pears in the title role. The relationship between Glyndebourne (my father, in particular) and the Britten 'camp'

1940	1941	1942	1943	1944
The Beggar's Opera tour			Audrey sang Susanna in	Audrey and the children

was icy and remained so for the next 34 years. Following the two Britten operas in 1947, Glyndebourne mounted a new production of Gluck's *Orfeo*, directed by Ebert, with Kathleen Ferrier making her debut in the eponymous role.

These exploits in Sussex were however overshadowed in terms of long-term magnitude by the start of the Edinburgh Festival in 1947. My father had invested a great deal of money in Glyndebourne before the war, and the prospects of recreating the Festival thereafter were financially daunting. Sponsorship as we now know it didn't exist in those days. My father searched in vain for people and companies to share the burden. My mother sowed the seed for a solution to this impasse by suggesting that Edinburgh would be an ideal venue for a festival. This seed germinated and inspired my father and Bing to look into moving the financial burden of Glyndebourne's continuation onto the shoulders of a newly founded festival elsewhere. My father befriended Sir John Falconer, Provost of Edinburgh, who had the vision to see the benefits which an international festival in his city could bring to the area. Against some odds, he successfully persuaded the 'City Fathers' to back the idea, and so the Edinburgh Festival was born. Glyndebourne, under Bing's authoritative and experienced administration, managed it from our Baker Street office until about three weeks before the Festival, when the Glyndebourne office moved up to Edinburgh in 1947. This continued to be the pattern of operation for the following two years, during which time there were no Festivals at Glyndebourne.

Just after the war, there was a dearth of cultural activity – there were other priorities. Edinburgh was like a lamp to moths, attracting the greatest performers of the day (the Vienna Philharmonic with Bruno Walter, Artur Schnabel, Pierre Fournier and Yehudi Menuhin, etc.), hungry for exposure in a showcase of the kind which Edinburgh offered. Glyndebourne and Bing provided the focus, direction and administrative know-how in the creation of the Festival. My father's bacon was for the time being saved, and Edinburgh's eggs hatched.

In 1947 *Macbeth* and *Figaro* represented Glyndebourne's operatic contribution, with Margherita Grandi (Lady Macbeth), Italo Tajo (Figaro), Giulietta Simionato (Cherubino), John Brownlee (the Count) and Eleanor Steber (the Countess) being the most well-known artists. Georg Szell should have conducted both productions, but without explanation or excuse disappeared (much to Bing's and my parents' chagrin) after a few days of rehearsal, and substitute conductors, Berthold Goldschmidt and Walter Susskind, were engaged in the 'nick of time'.

In the spring of 1948 Glyndebourne gave birth to and administered the Bath Festival, in which it mounted a production of *Die Entführung aus dem Serail*. But Bath was not a success. My father described the host city as 'dozy', and all thought of future plans there were abandoned.

In August that year Glyndebourne continued to manage the Edinburgh Festival and staged two productions directed by Ebert; *Don Giovanni*, with Rafael Kubelik conducting and, most notably, Ljuba Welitsch as Donna Anna, Paolo Silveri as the Don and Richard Lewis as Don Ottavio; and *Così* with the conductor Vittorio Gui, who was starting his long and productive association with Glyndebourne, and a stellar cast containing Erich Kunz (Guglielmo), Mariano Stabile (Alfonso), Suzanne Danco (Fiordiligi) and Hilde Güden (Despina).

In 1949 Bing was invited to become General Manager of the Metropolitan Opera House in New York, a job which he took up following the end of the Edinburgh Festival that year. His two assistants, Moran Caplat and Ian Hunter, were then appointed as General Managers of Glyndebourne and Edinburgh respectively.

Glyndebourne staged in Edinburgh that year a new production, directed by Ebert, of Verdi's *Un ballo in maschera* with Gui conducting, as well as a revival of *Così*, with Sena Jurinac (Dorabella) making her remarkable debut with the company.

Glyndebourne's fortunes were at this point taking a turn for the better, and …

1945 — End of the Second World War

1946 — Britten's *The Rape of Lucretia*

1947 — First Edinburgh Festival

1948

1949 — Moran Caplat succeeded Rudolf Bing as General Manager

ABOVE: Rudolf Bing beside the lake at Glyndebourne with two of the flamingoes in winter 1941. That year Mr Harvey wrote to Audrey, who was in Canada, that 'the flamingoes seem to be doing quite well now, although they do not look at home in our surroundings'

RIGHT: Mr Harvey working in the Rose Garden which had been turned over to the growing of vegetables for the war effort

The Beggar's Opera, directed by John Gielgud and designed by Motley, 1940.

ABOVE: Michael Redgrave as Macheath with Eugenie Walmsley as Jenny Diver (ANGUS McBEAN)

OPPOSITE: Roy Henderson, Audrey Mildmay and Constance Willis as the Peachums (ANGUS McBEAN)

SCENE FROM "THE BEGGAR'S OPERA"

Angus McBean
London.

ROY HENDERSON

CONSTANCE WILLIS

Audrey Mildmay

ROY HENDERSON — MR. PEACHUM
CONSTANCE WI[LLIS — M]RS. PEACHUM
[AUDREY MIL]DMAY — POLLY PEACHUM
(IN "THE BEGGAR'S OPERA")

ABOVE LEFT: Publicity photograph of Audrey and the children in Canada

ABOVE RIGHT: Rosamond and George home again at Glyndebourne, playing in one of the evacuee nurseries

OPPOSITE: Departure of Audrey and the children to Canada: (left to right) Rosamond, governess Miss Morgan, Audrey, Iona Tottenham (Audrey's god-daughter), George (obscured) and Admiral Sir Francis Tottenham, 1940

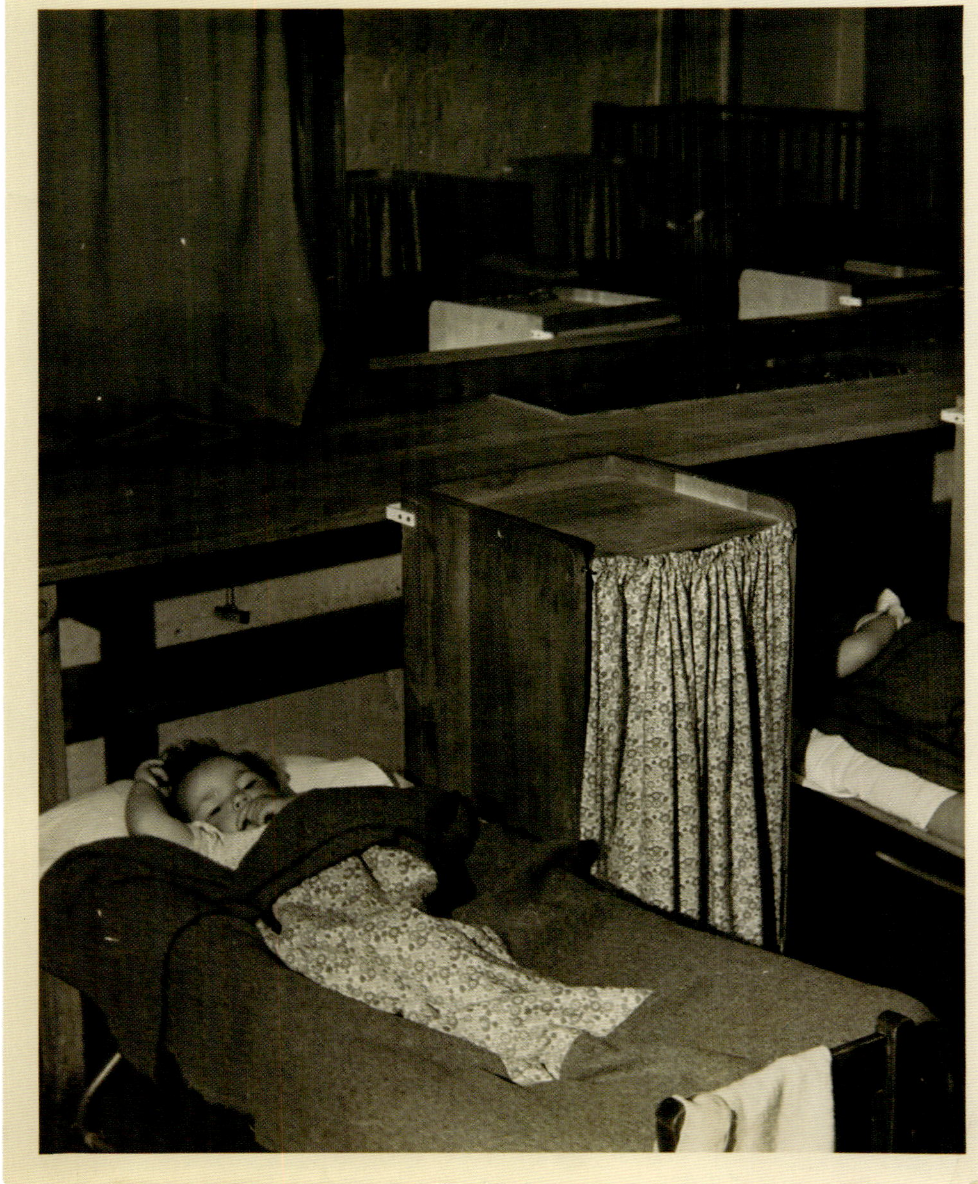

Evacuee children at Glyndebourne

Glyndebourne assumed the management of the Children's Theatre in 1945. It presented extensive tours of productions in their original form, rather than having them specially re-written for children. By the end of its second year, it had played to more than 250,000 children.

ABOVE: Audience at Toynbee Hall

OPPOSITE: *Everyman* tour, 1947: Peter Stephens (Strength), Jean McConnell (Five Wits), Rachel Order (Discretion), Susan Kennaway (Beauty), June Monkhouse (Knowledge), Margaret Leana (Good Deeds) and Donald Eccles (Everyman) (JOHN VICKERS)

The Rape of Lucretia, 1946.

LEFT: Ernst Ansermet, Benjamin Britten and Eric Crozier in the Walled Garden (ERICH AUERBACH)

BELOW: Nancy Evans and Frederick Sharp outside the Green Room

OPPOSITE TOP: Benjamin Britten, Ronald Duncan and John Piper in the Walled Garden, with a member of the music staff

OPPOSITE BOTTOM: Edmund Donlevy, Frank Rogier, Frederick Sharp and Owen Brannigan outside the Christie Dining Hall

The Rape of Lucretia, 1946.

ABOVE: A tea break during rehearsals. Top step; Catherine Lawson, Frank Rogier and Flora Nielsen. Lower steps; Nancy Evans, Lesley Duff, Frederick Sharp and Aksel Schiøtz

BELOW: Hans Schneider (costume maker), Eric Crozier, John Piper (designer), Margaret Ritchie and Catherine Lawson in the shrouded auditorium during rehearsals

OPPOSITE TOP: Flora Nielsen (Female Chorus) in her dressing room

OPPOSITE BOTTOM: Frank Rogier (Tarquinius) with Nancy Evans (Lucretia) in her dressing room

ABOVE: The visit of Queen Mary and Princess Alice to a performance of *The Rape of Lucretia*, July 18th,1946

BELOW: Final curtain call with John Christie and Benjamin Britten on stage together (GEORGE RODGER)

OPPOSITE TOP: Ernst Ansermet rehearsing the second cast of *The Rape of Lucretia* in the Organ Room, 1946. Britten at the piano with, at the end of the piano, Aksel Schiøtz (Male Chorus), Flora Nielsen (Female Chorus), Otakar Kraus (first cast Tarquinius) and Nancy Evans (Lucretia). The onlookers are, L to R: Norman Walker (Collatinus), Owen Brannigan (first cast Collatinus) seated, Catherine Lawson (Bianca), Peter Pears (first cast Male Chorus), and, with her back to the camera, Leslie Duff (Lucia) (ERICH AUERBACH)

OPPOSITE BOTTOM: The rape of Lucretia: Flora Nielsen (Female Chorus), Kathleen Ferrier (Lucretia), Frank Rogier (Tarquinius) and Aksel Schiøtz (Male Chorus), 1946 (ANGUS McBEAN)

Orfeo, 1947. Glyndebourne's first fully promoted production post-war – with Kathleen Ferrier making her debut in the title role. (ANGUS McBEAN)

KINGS
Proprietors: HOWARD & WYNDHAM, LTD
Chairman & Managing Director: A. STEWART CRUIKSHANK.
at
KING'S THEATRE
EDINBURGH
THE EDINBURGH FESTIVAL SOCIETY LTD.
GLYNDEBOURNE OPERA
EVENINGS AT 7 O'CLOCK
VERDI
UN BALLO IN MASCHERA
MOZART
GUI
CARL
HANS OPPENHEIM
IRENE EISINGER
ALDA NONI
LJUBA WELITSCH
JOHN BROWNLEE
MIRTO PICCHI
PAOLO SILVERI
ROYAL PHILHARMONIC

Inspired by Audrey's comment in 1940, 'What a place for a festival!', the Christies and Rudolf Bing co-founded, with the 'City Fathers', the Edinburgh Festival in 1947.

ABOVE: The ball scene from Glyndebourne's new production of Verdi's *Un ballo in maschera*, with Alda Noni as the Page and Mirto Picchi as Riccardo, 1947. This was one of only two new operas for Edinburgh which never transferred to Glyndebourne, the other being *La forza del destino* (ANGUS McBEAN)

OPPOSITE: Outside the King's Theatre, Edinburgh, for the 1947 Edinburgh Festival: Carl Ebert, Ljuba Welitsch and Mirto Picchi (MALCOLM DUNBAR)

1947 Edinburgh Festival, a revival of Glyndebourne's pre-war production of *Macbeth*.

ABOVE: Italo Tajo as Banquo with George Christie as Fleance (ANGUS McBEAN)

OPPOSITE: The Refugees chorus (ANGUS McBEAN)

ABOVE: Carl Ebert, John Christie, Audrey Mildmay and Fritz Stiedry (conductor of *Orfeo*), 1947

OPPOSITE: Suzanne Danco as Fiordiligi and Sena Jurinac as Dorabella, *Così fan tutte*, 1949

CBP 297
5433

Opera-goers picnicking in the car park at Glyndebourne, 1946 (GEORGE RODGER)

1950s

... the search for support materialised. Moran Caplat, the new General Manager, negotiated underwriting provided by a long-standing Glyndebourne enthusiast, Spedan Lewis of the John Lewis Partnership, amounting to £12,500, sufficient to meet the deficit on the rebirth of the Festival on its home ground.

So 1950 saw the company's homecoming but also marked the particularly welcome return of Fritz Busch for the first time since the war to conduct *Entführung* and *Così*, in which Jurinac transferred from Dorabella the year before to Fiordiligi with deafening and endless applause. A third production, *Figaro*, was also staged at Glyndebourne that year, with the Met baritone, George London, in the title role.

Glyndebourne was still attracting international singers including Erich Kunz (Guglielmo), who was in the Chorus before the war and had become a hot property in Vienna, Blanche Thebom (Dorabella), a mezzo star at the Met, and Alda Noni (Blonde and Despina), the best 'soubrette' of her day who had already sung Oscar the year before for Glyndebourne.

In August 1950 Glyndebourne, which had released its grip on the management of the Edinburgh Festival, returned there with a revival of *Figaro* and a new production – by Ebert (as ever) – of Strauss's *Ariadne auf Naxos* in its first version with Miles Malleson as M. Jourdain (a *nouveau riche sans pareil*) in his adapted and foreshortened take on Molière's *Le Bourgeois Gentilhomme* as the prologue to the opera. This was the only time that Beecham conducted an opera for Glyndebourne, despite countless meetings, negotiations and abortive plans with him in the post-war years. (He was even a tenant on the Glyndebourne Estate at the time.) *Ariadne* also brought Glyndebourne together with the designer Oliver Messel for the first time which presaged the start of a long

1950

1951

Death of Fritz Busch

Festival of Sussex

Idomeneo had its first professional production in the UK

1952

Glyndebourne Festival programme book started

1953

Death of Audrey Mildmay

The Rake's Progress first professional stage performance in the UK

1954

Formation of the Glyndebourne Arts Trust

Arlecchino given its first stage production in the UK

and productive association with this artist, consisting of eight productions in all.

Over the next four years, three significant developments occurred affecting Glyndebourne's financial well-being. Firstly, in 1951 the Treasury splashed out on a considerable grant for the Festival of Britain, £25,000 of which was voted for the Glyndebourne Festival that year – and for that year only. The Glyndebourne Festival has never received a penny of public money since. (In the late 1960s I had a meeting to persuade Lord Goodman, Chairman of the Arts Council, and Lord Harewood, Chairman of its Music Panel, to give grant-aid to the Festival, but the request was refused, largely on the grounds that such subsidy would help the 'wealthy elite' to attend our performances. The only way round this problem was to reduce seat prices and let in a wider audience, but this would then result in a need for greater subsidy out of proportion with the return on Government expenditure. Looking back at this unsuccessful endeavour, I thank my luck that the Festival retained and has always maintained its independence.)

1951 saw the first professional production of Mozart's *Idomeneo* in Britain, with Busch, Ebert and Messel – and Jurinac singing the most sublime Ilia I have ever heard or am likely to hear, Birgit Nilsson (Electra) giving her only performances with the Glyndebourne company, Richard Lewis (Idomeneo) guaranteeing much of his future career at Glyndebourne, and Léopold Simoneau (Idamante), in my view the finest Mozart tenor other than Fritz Wunderlich. Simoneau also sang Don Ottavio in *Don Giovanni* that year. The applause at the end of 'Il mio tesoro' was always prolonged. Geraint Evans made his debut at Glyndebourne as Masetto, and Lisa Della Casa was a delectable Countess in *Figaro*.

Glyndebourne was invited back to Edinburgh in 1951, where it repeated *Don Giovanni* and mounted another new production of a Verdi opera, *La forza del destino*, with Ebert and Busch – the last appearance that Busch made with Glyndebourne.

In September of that year he died, having contributed massively to a pivotal chapter in Glyndebourne's history.

The second development in restructuring Glyndebourne's financial well-being was largely initiated by a Hungarian, Miki Sekers, who had settled in England shortly before the war and created with entrepreneurial success the West Cumberland Silk Mills. My father and Sekers were kindred spirits in their love of private enterprise and distaste for publicly funded dependence – and their love of opera. Sekers devised means by which Glyndebourne could generate more funds over and above Box Office receipts – on which my father's enterprise depended – by tapping into additional support from Glyndebourne's existing audience. Firstly, the Glyndebourne Festival Society, effectively the 'Friends of Glyndebourne' – the first of many such associations to be created by artistic organisations over many years thereafter across the country – was instituted, membership of which provided priority booking and, for Glyndebourne, valuable subscription income; and, secondly, the large programme book as we now know it, covering the whole Festival and producing valuable income from advertisements, was brought into existence.

With these initiatives, the 1952 Festival and Glyndebourne's future were set fair – and then even fairer by the start of its resurrection of Rossini's operas, resulting from Vittorio Gui's emergence as Busch's heir apparent. *La Cenerentola* that year was the start of the canon of Rossini operas to be staged by Glyndebourne under Gui's baton – with the baritones Sesto Bruscantini and Ian Wallace together with the tenor Juan Oncina featuring prominently in these productions.

In a revival of *Idomeneo* in 1952, John Pritchard (already a member of the music staff) took over from the late Fritz Busch as conductor – the start of a long association with Glyndebourne, culminating in his appointment as Music Director in 1969.

In 1952, Glyndebourne was replaced at the Edinburgh Festival by the Hamburg State Opera, which caused some chagrin in Scotland.

My mother died on May 31st, 1953, a week before the opening of the Festival. She was the spirit of inspiration behind my father. She had the wholehearted trust and confidence of Busch and Ebert and provided an all-pervasive glow to Glyndebourne's working conditions. Her legacy was an abiding goal for perfectionism achieved with heart and practicality.

Gluck's *Alceste* was the new production at Glyndebourne that year, but it is Stravinsky's *The Rake's Progress* in Glyndebourne's return to the Edinburgh Festival which sticks most strongly in the memory (particularly for me, because I was a producer's assistant on it). This was its British premiere, directed by Ebert, who had staged the work's world premiere two years earlier in Venice, while Osbert Lancaster was the inspired choice of designer. *The Rake* has been in Glyndebourne's repertoire ever since and is due to return in 2010.

The third development in securing Glyndebourne's long-term future was the establishment in 1954 of the Glyndebourne Arts Trust, the first charity of its kind. The performing arts as such were not considered at the time to merit charitable status. My mother expressed considerable anxiety about the formation of this Trust, on the grounds that the family might lose artistic control in the process. She was won over, and after a lengthy struggle with the Charity Commission and lobbying of some senior Government ministers, charitable status was

granted – and set a precedent for, and was and has been copied by, a huge number of performing companies in the country.

The 1954 season opened with a new production of *Il barbiere di Siviglia*, with Gui flying Rossini's banner with a loving and immaculate flourish. In a perfectly balanced cast, Graziella Sciutti was a consummate Rosina. A new production by Ebert's son, Peter, of Busoni's enchanting *Arlecchino* (its first professional staging in the UK) was also mounted in 1954 as a curtain-raiser for *Ariadne* (second version with the prologue) conducted by Pritchard who was by now a regular performer with the company. Solti made his UK debut in *Don Giovanni*. He failed to 'click' with Glyndebourne and we failed to 'click' with him. We missed a trick, as we were soon to learn when he became the Royal Opera House's chief conductor.

The following year was mainly notable for the introduction of Rossini's *Le Comte Ory*, barely known in the UK; and for a new production of Verdi's *Falstaff* with Geraint Evans (a regular performer with the company) making his debut in the title role with resounding applause in Glyndebourne's last appearance at the Edinburgh Festival – except for a one-off visit in 1960. Carlo Maria Giulini made his UK debut in this production, but his success did not endear him to Gui, and this, it seems to me, is the only reason we were unable to re-engage him. We missed another trick.

1956 was the bicentenary of Mozart's birth, which Glyndebourne celebrated by performing a new production of *Die Zauberflöte* and revivals of the three da Ponte operas (with Joan Sutherland as the Countess in *Figaro*), and of *Idomeneo* and *Die Entführung*.

The following year saw new productions of Rossini's *L'italiana in Algeri*, with Peter Ebert directing in designs by Lancaster, and of Mozart's one-acter, *Der Schauspieldirektor*, directed by Carl Ebert's assistant, Anthony Besch, as the curtain-raiser to *Ariadne*, in which Elisabeth Söderström took over the role of the Composer with thunderous applause, which had until then been (among many roles at Glyndebourne) the preserve of Jurinac.

In the context of repertory, 1958 was even lighter on novelty, with only one new operatic introduction, namely Wolf-Ferrari's *Il segreto di Susanna*, directed by Peter Ebert and preceding *Ariadne*. The other new introduction was Mary into my family. We married in 1958 – and I didn't know then anything like the extent of my luck.

1959 was an artistic turning point. Carl Ebert, in his last year as Artistic Director, created with Messel an overwhelmingly wonderful *Rosenkavalier* with a trio of ladies – Régine Crespin as the Marschallin, Söderström as Octavian and Anneliese Rothenberger as Sophie vying with the famous pre-war trio of Schumann, Lehmann and Olczwska. Günther Rennert, Ebert's successor, staged *Fidelio* with Gui conducting a deeply moving performance and Gré Brouwenstijn and Richard Lewis as the totally convincing protagonists.

By 1959 Ebert, over the 19 years Glyndebourne had been in full operation on home territory and in Edinburgh, had staged 20 out of 21 full-length operas. You can hardly be more of a mainstay. A pupil of Max Reinhardt and an actor/director of huge account in Germany, he was the answer to a prayer for my parents and, as I said in my chapter on the 1930s, he brought a new dimension to operatic production in this country over a wide variety of repertory. He was a cornerstone in Glyndebourne's artistic edifice.

Glyndebourne was on the point of entering …

ABOVE: The unchanging profile of the tree-lined hill behind the car park, 1951 (R RILKES)

OPPOSITE: Sheep grazing in the chalk landscape surrounding Glyndebourne, 1954 (GUY GRAVETT)

LEFT: Karel Horitz, a cellist with the Royal Philharmonic Orchestra, cycles into Glyndebourne in evening dress and with his cello strapped to his back. John Christie is seen in the background, 1951 (CORNELL CAPA)
ABOVE: Sequence of images showing members of the Royal Philharmonic Orchestra playing croquet during the long interval, 1958 (HERB GREER)

AME 626
ERK
915

B.B.C.

A BBC Outside Broadcast Unit came to Glyndebourne for the first time on July 23rd, 1951, when a special performance of *Così fan tutte* was broadcast live. In addition to seeing the opera, viewers saw scenes of the gardens and interviews with distinguished guests. Three centimetric wave radio link stations were set up on the high points along the route to London to transmit the signal to Alexandra Palace.

TOP: One of the CPS emitron cameras on a specially built scaffold tower in the gardens

ABOVE: Rooney Pelletier interviewing John Christie in the Organ Room for the broadcast

OPPOSITE TOP: The first radio link station on top of the Downs above Glyndebourne

OPPOSITE BOTTOM: One of the mobile control rooms parked in the driveway outside Glyndebourne

TOP: Interior of the auditorium with the designer Hugh Casson on stage on the set for *Alceste*, his first design for Glyndebourne, 1953

ABOVE: Back view of the theatre from the Walled Garden, 1953 (REEVES)

Preparations for the visit to Paris, 1958, top to bottom: Oliver Messel on the set for *Le Comte Ory*; Preparing costumes in the wardrobe department; *Le Comte Ory* Fernando Cadoni, Sari Barabas, Juan Oncina; Graziella Sciutti as Nannetta; Rosemary Vercoe working in the props department; Moran Caplat and Jani Strasser in the Green Room; Heinz Blankenberg; Geraint Evans in a break from rehearsals; chief dresser Nellie Ayers; Members of the *Falstaff* cast (Fernanda Cadoni, Ilva Ligabue and Graziella Sciutti) in the Green Room; Ilva Ligabue, Graziella Sciutti, Fernanda Cadoni playing croquet (JOHN HEDGECOE)

ABOVE: A rehearsal on stage for *Die Entführung aus dem Serail*. Carl Ebert with Richard Holm as Belmonte, Endre Koréh as Osmin and Murray Dickie as Pedrillo, 1950 (ROGER WOOD)

OPPOSITE TOP: Carl Ebert taking a *Falstaff* rehearsal on stage. Mario Borriello as Ford, Geraint Evans as Falstaff and Oralia Dominguez as Mistress Quickly, 1958 (GUY GRAVETT)

OPPOSITE BOTTOM: *Arlecchino* designed by Peter Rice, 1954. Mr R Jones as the donkey driver, Geraint Evans as Abbate Cospicuo, Fritz Ollendorf as Doctor Bombasto, Murray Dickie as Leandro, Douglas Craig and Reg Cornish from stage management as the back and front ends of the donkey, and Elaine Malbin as Colombina (GUY GRAVETT)

ABOVE: Wardrobe Mistress Rosemary Vercoe, director Carl Ebert and designer Osbert Lancaster at a costume parade for *The Rake's Progress* in the Green Room. Peter Ebert can be seen seated on the left, 1953 (GUY GRAVETT)

OPPOSITE: The dancer Sylvia Ebert, wife of Peter Ebert, in the Green Room during a break in rehearsals, 1953 (GUY GRAVETT)

Falstaff, directed by Carl Ebert and designed by Osbert Lancaster.

ABOVE: Geraint Evans as Falstaff, 1957 (ANGUS McBEAN)

OPPOSITE: Graziella Sciutti as Nannetta, 1958 (GUY GRAVETT)

ABOVE: Geraint Evans as Papageno and Pilar Lorengar as Pamina in *Die Zauberflöte*, 1956 (SNOWDON)

OPPOSITE TOP: Sesto Bruscantini (Figaro), Ian Wallace (Bartolo), Graziella Sciutti (Rosina) and Juan Oncina (Almaviva), *Il barbiere di Siviglia*, 1954 (GUY GRAVETT)

OPPOSITE BOTTOM: Sena Jurinac (Ilia), Richard Lewis (Idomeneo), Leopold Simoneau (Idamante) and Birgit Nilsson (Electra), *Idomeneo*, 1951 (ANGUS McBEAN)

All three productions were directed by Carl Ebert and designed by Oliver Messel.

The Rake's Progress at the Edinburgh Festival: directed by Carl Ebert and designed by Osbert Lancaster.

TOP: Richard Lewis (Tom Rakewell) and Jerome Hines (Nick Shadow), 1953 (GUY GRAVETT)

ABOVE: Richard Lewis (Tom Rakewell) and Marina de Gabarain (Baba the Turk) with the Glyndebourne Chorus outside Tom's house, 1954 (GUY GRAVETT)

OPPOSITE: *Don Giovanni*, with Richard Lewis as Don Ottavio and Sena Jurinac as Donna Anna in the production directed by Carl Ebert and designed by John Piper, 1955 (GUY GRAVETT)

Der Rosenkavalier, directed by Carl Ebert and designed by Oliver Messel, 1959. Elisabeth Söderström as Octavian, Régine Crespin as the Marschallin and Anneliese Rothenburger as Sophie (GUY GRAVETT)

ABOVE: *Der Schauspieldirektor*, directed by Anthony Besch and designed by Peter Rice. Joan Sutherland as Madame Herz in this curtain-raiser to *Ariadne auf Naxos*, 1957 (GUY GRAVETT)

OPPOSITE: Alda Noni (Clorinda), Ian Wallace (Don Magnifico) and Fernanda Cadoni (Tisbe) in *La Cenerentola*, directed by Carl Ebert and designed by Oliver Messel, 1953 (ANGUS McBEAN)

Guy Gravett

ABOVE: Anna Pollak as Dorabella, Alda Noni as Despina, Dezsö Ernster as Don Alfonso, Sena Jurinac as Fiordiligi, Sesto Bruscantini as Guglielmo and Richard Lewis as Ferrando in *Così fan tutte*, 1952 (GUY GRAVETT)
OPPOSITE: Dorothy MacNeil (Cherubino) with Lisa Della Casa (Countess) in *Le nozze di Figaro*, 1951 (GUY GRAVETT)
Both productions were directed by Carl Ebert. Design for *Così fan tutte* was by Rolf Gérard and for *Le nozze di Figaro* by Hutchinson Scott (sets) and Rolf Gérard (costumes).

ABOVE: On the terrace, 1951: Fritz Busch, John Christie, Carl Ebert and Moran Caplat (ROGER WOOD)
BELOW: Music staff meeting, 1957: Paul Hamburger, Bryan Balkwill, Paul Sacher, Martin Isepp, Dennis Wicks, Jani Strasser, Ellen Thurman and Peter Gellhorn (GUY GRAVETT)
OPPOSITE: John Christie addressing the company from the stage, 1950 (CORNELL CAPA)

TOP: John Christie escorts Princess Margaret along the platform at Lewes Station, with Audrey Christie following behind, 1948

ABOVE: The Queen and Princess Margaret with John Christie at Glyndebourne on a visit to see *Le nozze di Figaro*, June 30th, 1956

OPPOSITE TOP: Lunch in the staff dining room, June 22nd, 1951, (the original Christie Dining Hall), Moran Caplat, Carl Ebert, John Christie and Fritz Busch (CORNELL CAPA)

OPPOSITE BOTTOM: Audrey and John Christie talking with members of the audience, June 22nd, 1951 (CORNELL CAPA)

HP

ABOVE: George and Mary Christie on their wedding day, August 8th, 1958, with bridesmaids Camilla Gage and Tessa Bridgeman (ROGER WOOD)

OPPOSITE: Mary Nicholson before her marriage to George Christie (SNOWDON)

ABOVE: Opera-goers dur ng the interval in the car park, June 1951 (CORNELL CAPA)

OPPOSITE: A couple pic nicking in the grounds, 1959 (ERICH AUERBACH)

ABOVE: Before the performance, 1955 (JANE BOWN)

OPPOSITE: Members of the audience in the gardens, 1953 (HENRI CARTIER-BRESSON)

1960s

... into a new era with mixed fortune. Gui remained much in evidence and in 1960 was granted his abiding wish for Glyndebourne to stage an opera by Bellini, a composer he had championed in Italy. *I puritani*, starring Joan Sutherland, opened the Festival that year, with Gui's stepson Franco Enriquez directing. (Some eight years before, Gui and Enriquez had teamed up at Covent Garden when Callas made her memorable debut in this country singing Norma.) As it turned out, *Puritani* was the only Bellini opera to be staged by Glyndebourne. I've always rather longed to do *Beatrice di Tenda*.

Don Giovanni was staged by Rennert, in which Mirella Freni (Zerlina) started her association with Glyndebourne, and Ebert revived four of his productions – one of which, *Die Zauberflöte*, was conducted by Colin Davis. Sadly, it was the only opera he performed with Glyndebourne. He replaced Beecham who, through ill health, had to cancel in the final twilight of his years.

Glyndebourne then went back to the Edinburgh Festival for the first time in five years – and for the last time ever – with revivals of *Falstaff* and *Puritani*, together with a triple bill consisting of *Il segreto di Susanna* and *Arlecchino* from stock and Poulenc's *La Voix humaine*, with Pritchard conducting, Denise Duval, for whom the solo role had been written, and Jean Cocteau directing and designing. It centres on a girl who spends a great deal of time on the telephone trying desperately to rescue her love affair. I witnessed a row in rehearsals between Miss Duval, who was insisting on a prompter, and Cocteau, who was adamantly resisting this idea. The Head of Music Staff

1960

Günther Rennert succeeded Carl Ebert as Artistic Director

1961

Birth of Hector Thomas Cleveland Christie

World premiere in original language of *Elegy for Young Lovers*

1962

Death of John Christie

L'incoronazione di Poppea had its first professional production in the UK

1963

Birth of Augustus Jack Christie (Gus)

1964

tapped her elbow and whispered to her that, whenever she was in need of help, he would be at the other end of the phone ...

The following year, 1961, was notable for a new production of Donizetti's *L'elisir d'amore*, directed and designed by Franco Zeffirelli – his one and only production for Glyndebourne – and for the world premiere of Hans Werner Henze's *Elegy for Young Lovers* to a libretto by Auden and Kallman, with Pritchard conducting and Rennert directing. Zeffirelli's *L'elisir* was a rustic concoction of perfection, a definitive presentation of Donizetti's enchanting comedy, while *Elegy* was most memorable for Lila de Nobili's stunning and atmospheric design of a single set. It was at a performance of *Elegy* that my father was heard to say, when asked by a member of the audience where the Friesian cows had gone in the field next to the ha-ha, 'Oh, they'll be back tomorrow when Mozart's *Don Giovanni* is in performance ...'

1961 marked the first occasion that the BBC Proms at the Albert Hall broke with tradition and engaged an opera company, namely Glyndebourne, to perform a full-length work. *Don Giovanni*, after a run of 13 performances at Glyndebourne, was given in a semi-staged performance without scenery and costumes and was the start of an association with the BBC at the Proms which has persisted every year since. This was part of Glyndebourne's strategy to reach out to wider audiences, pioneered with its pre-war recordings with HMV, and the television recordings of its productions by the BBC dating back to 1951. *Così* was the first non-BBC produced opera to be transmitted on screen.

1962 was a momentous year that witnessed the end of an era and the start of a new line of repertory.

In mid-season my father died aged 79. Glyndebourne had been his and my mother's brainchild. His identification with and devotion to Glyndebourne were total. His single-minded resolve to make it a success and maintain its position on the world's operatic stage were Glyndebourne's *raison d'être*. His eccentricities brought a strong sense of character to the direction he gave the company's development and enduring independence.

The season opened with Debussy's *Pelléas et Mélisande* in a production designed unforgettably by Beni Montresor, recommended by Lila de Nobili, who was unable to take on the task. It was directed by Ebert, making a guest appearance – having given up his Artistic Directorship in 1959 – and making his last indelibly memorable appearance at Glyndebourne. Gui conducted and Denise Duval was *Mélisande*. I don't ever expect to see or hear a more atmospherically hypnotic performance of this enigmatic and impressionist opera (Graham Vick's production in 1999 vied with Ebert's).

But it was Monteverdi's *L'incoronazione di Poppea* which gave a huge impetus in taking Glyndebourne down a new and almost totally uncharted route. Raymond Leppard, who had been on the music staff in the mid-1950s, created an epoch-change to our appreciation of early Italian opera which, on the whole, lay wholesale gathering dust on the shelves of La Biblioteca Marciano in Venice and elsewhere. Many efforts had been made to revive this repertoire, but none had truly grasped a response from a wide audience. Leppard brought these early operas to life by charging the veins of his orchestral arrangements with red corpuscles which others had failed to provide – arguing that, had the composers of these early operas had the orchestral forces available to them that were now at his disposal in the 20th century, they would have exploited this wealth of musical development. This, in the course of time, has been his undoing, as the purists have imposed their will on the prevailing style of performance of this early music. But it was without a shadow of doubt Leppard who woke audiences up to this repertoire and put it back on the map – and Glyndebourne, over the next decade, gave him the showcase in which to do this.

Poppea was a 'hot-ticket' in 1962, but the revival of *L'elisir* with Freni, Bruscantini and Luigi Alva – a dream cast – was, in its more populist way, jockeying for position.

1965

1966

Birth of Patricia Louise Christie

1967

First performances of *L'Ormindo* since 1644

1968

Glyndebourne Touring Opera made its inaugural tour

1969

John Pritchard appointed as Music Director

My father's packed-out funeral in Westminster Abbey in September, with Quintin Hailsham making the address, and the Royal Philharmonic Orchestra (Glyndebourne's resident orchestra) together with Glyndebourne soloists performing the *Mozart Requiem*, saw out the end of a creative era which brought huge uplift to the world of opera. For the next few years Glyndebourne might be described as undergoing a period of recreation. Gui, though still active, was in some measure handing over his musical reins as Glyndebourne's chief conductor to Pritchard, Rennert was Head of Productions, Caplat was the Chief Executive; Jani Strasser (originally my mother's singing teacher in Vienna) had carved out an indispensable position for himself as head of music and casting director; and I was tagging along behind learning the trade.

Capriccio and *Die Zauberflöte* were the two new productions in 1963. *Capriccio* – directed by Rennert and conducted by Pritchard with, most memorably, Söderström as the Countess and Tom Krause as the Count – survived for 35 years in Glyndebourne's repertoire in the architectural one-act set designed by Dennis Lennon, albeit redecorated by Martin Battersby in John Cox's brilliantly re-thought production of 1973. No other set for a production has lasted so long at Glyndebourne, though Cox's production in David Hockney's definitive sets of *The Rake's Progress* looks set fair to challenge this longevity.

Zauberflöte was conducted by Gui, directed by his stepson Enriquez (a flirtation which then developed between him and Glyndebourne over the next few years), and designed by Emanuele Luzzati in sets of simple and flexible ingenuity which consisted of ten mobile columns vertically triangular in shape, with each of the three facets containing a different visual theme. The choreographed movement of these columns against back-drops matching the changing facets provided the location of the scenes. Luzzati's input represented the biggest break with theatrical design conventions at Glyndebourne at that time.

1964 was an undistinguished year, with the new regime showing weakness in direction and leadership. New productions were Verdi's *Macbeth*, memorable principally for Kostas Paskali's riveting account of the title role, and Rossini's *La pietra del paragone*, forgettable on account of the absence of any saving grace. There was, however, a moment of glory created in the revival of *Idomeneo* in which Luciano Pavarotti sang Idamante (the only Mozart role in his career until he came to sing Idamante's father, Idomeneo, many years later at the New York Met) and Gundula Janowitz was a serene Ilia.

In 1964, the Royal Philharmonic Orchestra, which had performed in the Festival for some 16 years, was replaced by the London Philharmonic Orchestra, which has performed every year since that date. The loss of the RPO was occasioned more than anything by its lack of artistic direction following the death of Beecham, its Principal Conductor, in 1961 and the exodus of many of its best players to other orchestras offering better artistic and financial prospects. The fact that Pritchard was at the time taking over Gui's mantle at Glyndebourne and happened to be the Principal Conductor of the LPO reinforced Glyndebourne's resolve to make this major change.

1965 saw a further dip in Glyndebourne's artistic fortunes, with indifferent stagings of Cimarosa's *Il matrimonio segreto* and Donizetti's *Anna Bolena*, and too many high-profile cancellations and defections by soloists in four revivals (including Gui, Montserrat Caballé and Gérard Souzay from *Figaro* alone). And so it was that Glyndebourne radically rethought its operational policy and in 1966 mounted a totally reshaped Festival, consisting of four productions rather than the six which it was customarily presenting at the time. The announcement of this planned retreat was given short shrift in the press, which considered that it presaged the end of the Festival. The outcome of this hectic re-thinking process did nothing to allay the press's scaremongering. A double bill consisting of Purcell's *Dido and Aeneas* (with, thank heavens, Janet Baker as Dido) was staged in tandem with Ravel's *L'Heure espagnole*. You can't conceive a more ill-assorted pair of operas. *Werther*, directed by

Michael Redgrave, was the next new production in 1966 and didn't do much to raise the spirits (particularly mine, being lukewarm about Massenet). Handel's *Jephtha*, effectively a Rennert production imported from Hamburg, was the third novelty – a stylistically disastrous one in which *da capo* sections of arias were cut ... Richard Lewis – a Glyndebourne stalwart – Heather Harper, and Margaret Price in the tiny role of the Angel, helped a bit to mitigate the disaster. A revival of the Enriquez production of *Die Zauberflöte* was run-of-the-mill.

1967 continued with four productions, two of which were new: *Bohème*, directed by Redgrave, was a 'turkey' and Cavalli's *L'Ormindo*, directed by Rennert and conducted by Leppard, was a signal of recovery in Glyndebourne's time of artistic need. Rennert then resigned from Glyndebourne to become Intendant in Munich.

The 1968 Festival was principally memorable for Söderström's ravishing and touching performance of Tatyana in Tchaikovsky's *Eugene Onegin*. At the end of one performance Peter Hall approached me and said he wanted to come and work with us. His expression of interest quickened my pulse. I discussed the matter with Moran Caplat, the General Administrator, and the Board, the up-shot of which led to Glyndebourne's offer of the role of Artistic Director to Hall, who at the time was leaving the Royal Shakespeare Company (which he created) and was beginning to get into films. Some months passed and I received a telegram from him, effectively saying that his film work was not coming good, and he had received an offer from the Royal Opera House to join Colin Davis and John Tooley as the triumvirate which would provide the artistic lifeblood to that institution. It was an offer which, given his circumstances at the time, was financially irresistible.

1968 was chiefly memorable for the start of Glyndebourne Touring Opera (GTO). For years Glyndebourne had been training up young singers as understudies in the Festival. More often than not, they never replaced their principals and were ready-made contractual 'fodder' for other companies (well, bugger that!). I was keen to provide a platform on which to exploit this talent and bring Glyndebourne's productions to a wider audience. After two years of negotiation with the Arts Council, we got just about enough subsidy – combined with help from the Gulbenkian Foundation and our regular

supporters – to launch the company. Brian Dickie, Caplat's assistant, and I were the prime movers behind the start of GTO, Dickie becoming the company's first Administrator. It has been and is an indispensable part of Glyndebourne's operation – and has been from 1968 until now – by far the most parsimoniously subsidised opera company of its size and output in the UK.

The decade ending in 1969 saw only one new production directed and designed by Enriquez and Luzzati, namely *Così*, with Margaret Price as Fiordiligi (the previous year she had sung Constanze robustly and beautifully in another Enriquez/Luzzati production, Mozart's *Die Entführung aus dem Serail*). Revivals that year saw Ileana Cotrubas make her Glyndebourne debut as a Mélisande *sans pareil* and Ruggero Raimondi as a Don Giovanni with charm – a characteristic rarely seen in the portrayal of this role nowadays.

The Glyndebourne Festival had been through a three-year trough, but ...

ABOVE LEFT: View of the house and terrace (GUY GRAVETT)

ABOVE RIGHT: A quiet corner of the garden (GUY GRAVETT)

OPPOSITE: Bust of John Christie in the Walled Garden, 1960s. Commissioned in 1959 by patrons and members of the company for Glyndebourne's 25th anniversary and sculpted by Oscar Nemon, it was presented to John Christie on stage at the final night of the 1960 Festival

85
86
87
88
91
92
93
94
95
96
SAFETY FILM
KODAK

ABOVE: *L'incoronazione di Poppea* rehearsal in the Ebert Room. Martin Isepp at the piano, with dancer Robert Harrold, Hugues Cuénod (Lucano) and director Günther Rennert, 1962 (GUY GRAVETT)

OPPOSITE: *Die Zauberflöte* rehearsal with conductor Vittorio Gui, designer Emanuele Luzzati and director Franco Enriquez, 1963 (GUY GRAVETT

25
26
27
28
29
30
31
32
33
34
35
36
KODAK
SAFETY FILM

ABOVE: Conductor Vittorio Gui during a rehearsal of *Pelléas et Mélisande*, 1963. Denise Duval (Mélisande) can be seen in the background (GUY GRAVETT)

OPPOSITE: Carl Ebert rehearsing Hans Wilbrink (Pelléas) and Michel Roux (Golaud) in *Pelléas et Mélisande*, 1963 (GUY GRAVETT)

ABOVE: *Elegy for Young Lovers* meeting in the Organ Room, 1961. Top left frame 57: librettists WH Auden and Chester Kallman, composer Hans Werner Henze and director Günther Rennert (GUY GRAVETT)

OPPOSITE: *Capriccio* rehearsal: Elisabeth Söderström, Günther Rennert, John Pritchard and Jani Strasser, 1963 (GUY GRAVETT)

59
63
67
60
64
61
65
69
62
66
70
KODAK
SAFETY FILM

ABOVE: The 1960 revival of *Falstaff* in typical designs by Osbert Lancaster with Mariella Adani as Nannetta (GUY GRAVETT)

OPPOSITE: Mariella Adani as Susanna and Sesto Bruscantini as Gil, *Il segreto di Susanna* at the Edinburgh Festival, directed by Peter Ebert and designed by Carl Toms, 1960

THE SCOTSMAN.
EDINBURGH

Die Zauberflöte, directed by Franco Enriquez and designed by Emanuele Luzzati, 1963

ABOVE: Heinz Blankenberg as Papageno (GUY GRAVETT)

OPPOSITE: Claudine Arnaud as the Queen of the Night (GUY GRAVETT)

L'incoronazione di Poppea, directed by Günther Rennert with a set designed by Hugh Casson and costumes by Joyce Conwy Evans, 1962.
TOP: Magda Laszlo as Poppea with Oralia Dominguez as Arnalta (GUY GRAVETT)
RIGHT: Carlo Cava as Seneca with his followers before his suicide (GUY GRAVETT)

OPPOSITE: John Wakefield as Ormindo, watches Anne Howells as Erisbe and Peter-Christoph Runge as Amida, *L'Ormindo*, directed by Günther Rennert and designed by Erich Kondrak, 1967 (GUY GRAVETT)

ABOVE: Joan Sutherland as Elvira, *I Puritani*, 1960 (GUY GRAVETT)

OPPOSITE: Elisabeth Söderström as the Countess, *Capriccio*, 1963 (GUY GRAVETT)

ABOVE: Kostas Paskalis as Macbeth, 1964 (GUY GRAVETT)

OPPOSITE: The apparitions scene from *Macbeth*: dress rehearsal with the London Philharmonic Orchestra in the pit, 1964 (GUY GRAVETT)

ABOVE: *Don Giovanni*, directed by Günther Rennert and designed by Ita Maximowna, 1960. Leonardo Monreale (Masetto), Mirella Freni (Zerlina), Ilva Ligabue (Donna Elvira), Geraint Evans (Leporello, dressed as the Don), Joan Sutherland (Donna Anna) and Richard Lewis (Don Ottavio) (GUY GRAVETT)
RIGHT: Luciano Pavarotti as Idamante, *Idomeneo*, 1964 (GUY GRAVETT)
OPPOSITE: Sesto Bruscantini as Leporello, *Don Giovanni*, 1960 (GUY GRAVETT)

ABOVE: Emanuele Luzzati painting scenery for *Die Zauberflöte*, the first of six operas he designed for Glyndebourne, 1963 (GUY GRAVETT)

OPPOSITE: Franco Zeffirelli working on the set model for *L'elisir d'amore*, 1961 (GUY GRAVETT)

ABOVE: The Christie family: George Christie (on sofa), John Christie (seated), Sock the pug dog, Mary Christie and Rosamond Christie standing, 1960 (GUY GRAVETT)

OPPOSITE TOP: Stage hand Bert Jackson, having a pint (GUY GRAVETT)

OPPOSITE BOTTOM: Janet Moores, Emanuele Luzzati and June Dandridge at supper. Janet Moores began working at Glyndebourne aged 15, before the establishment of the Festival, and went on to become House Manager and later, Accommodation Manager. She devoted more than 50 years of her life to Glyndebourne. June Dandridge joined Glyndebourne in 1951 as one of the first female stage managers in the UK, becoming Stage Director in 1956 with overall charge of the stage and all the technical departments. In 1960 she became Production Manager, the right-hand to the General Manager, Moran Caplat, until her retirement in 1986 (GUY GRAVETT)

Glyndebourne Touring Opera, spring 1968.

ABOVE LEFT: Music Director Myer Fredman with Administrator Brian Dickie on the set of *Die Zauberflöte,* preparing for the first tour (GUY GRAVETT)

ABOVE RIGHT: Richard Van Allan and Geoffrey Chard as Leporello and Don Giovanni, *Don Giovanni* (GUY GRAVETT)

OPPOSITE: Annon Lee Silver as Pamina and John Serge as Tamino, *Die Zauberflöte,* designed by Emanuele Luzzati (GUY GRAVETT)

DOTT.

Glyndebourne Touring Opera, 1968.

BELOW: *L'Ormindo*, the 'dead' lovers, with April Cantelo as Erisbe, John Wakefield as Ormindo, Anthony Williams as Ariadeno and Richard Van Allan as Osmano (GUY GRAVETT)

OPPOSITE TOP: Jill Gomez (Adina), Terence Sharpe (Belcore) and Ryland Davies (Nemorino), *L'elisir d'amore* (GUY GRAVETT)

OPPOSITE BOTTOM: Ian Wallace as Dulcamara, *L'elisir d'amore* (GUY GRAVETT)

ABOVE: Before the performance, 1960 (GUY GRAVETT)

OPPOSITE: The end of the lake seen through the willows, 1962 (GUY GRAVETT)

ABOVE: Audience on the Green Room lawn, 1967 (TONY RAY JONES)

OPPOSITE: A stroll through the Rose Garden, 1963 (GUY GRAVETT)

1970s

... the process of recovery at the start of the new decade began to be apparent. Five productions were staged in 1970 instead of the four to which Glyndebourne's reduced circumstances in 1966 had subjected the Festival.

Peter Hall had decided at the end of the 1960s to turn down the offer from the Royal Opera House and accepted instead the directorship of the National Theatre. This, thank heavens, freed him up in some degree for work at Glyndebourne – and what a breath of fresh air he brought to us.

The opening production of the 1970 Festival was Cavalli's *La Calisto*, directed by Hall, in designs by John Bury which were very much in the style of 17th-century Venetian theatre, while exploiting modern materials and stage techniques. Leppard, an old colleague of Hall from their undergraduate days at Cambridge, conducted, and the cast was led sublimely by Cotrubas as Calisto and Janet Baker as the goddess Diana, doubling with subtle comedy in disguise as the lascivious Jove. The reviews for this rarity were rhapsodic, and *Calisto* consolidated Glyndebourne's position as the leading pioneer in the rebirth of early Italian Baroque opera.

The other highlight in 1970 was the staging of Glyndebourne's first commissioned opera, Nicholas Maw's *The Rising of the Moon*, to an inventively comic libretto by Beverley Cross. Colin Graham directed the piece with imaginative sensitivity – sadly his only production for Glyndebourne. Modern comic operas are an extreme rarity, and on this account alone I am amazed that *The Rising of the Moon* has not been taken up extensively by other opera companies.

A third new production in this Festival, Rossini's *Turco in Italia*, featured Paolo Montarsolo and Graziella Sciutti –

1970

World premiere of Glyndebourne's first commissioned opera, *The Rising of the Moon*

First performance of

1971

Birth of Ivor Ptolemy Christie

1972

First British performance of *Il ritorno d'Ulisse in patria*

John Cox became Artistic Director

1973

1974

long-standing favourites of the Glyndebourne audience – heading the cast under the baton of John Pritchard, whose position, after almost two decades of conducting in the Festival, had been formalised in 1969 as Musical Director. This production was scheduled to be directed by the highly talented but capricious Franco Enriquez. Instead, at a very late date, John Cox, who had assisted on several productions over some ten years, took on the task – it was the start of a long and fruitful collaboration at Glyndebourne.

At the end of the 1970 season, Jani Strasser retired. Since 1934 he had held a key position at Glyndebourne, preparing the singers for performance and seemingly acting as a conduit between conductors and singers on the one part and the composer, with whom he had a direct line, on the other! He was also instrumental in discovering many of Glyndebourne's budding stars. Above all, he championed standards in vocal quality, interpretation and communication.

The 1971 Festival contained two new productions, Tchaikovsky's *The Queen of Spades* – a disappointment following the success of *Onegin* – and *Ariadne auf Naxos* in the second version with Strauss's Prologue. The setting remains a highlight in my memory, directed with theatrical ingenuity by Cox in what looked like the under-stage area of Drottningholm (the perfectly preserved 18th-century theatre adjoining the Swedish royal family's summer palace outside Stockholm), and designed by Michael Annals.

At this time Glyndebourne made the decision to swap its annual tour from the spring to the autumn. The Arts Council agreed to this, but seemed not to notice that in the process GTO halved the length of its tour in spring 1971, while receiving subsidy at the level it had got for its full-length tours. In the autumn of 1971, which for the Arts Council fell in a different financial year, GTO received the same subsidy for a foreshortened tour, thereby doubling its financial support in that calendar year. In 1972 Glyndebourne successfully argued its case for retention of this enhanced level of finance on resumption of its customary length of touring – a level which formed the basis of funding thereafter.

The programme in 1971, containing five productions, seems to have caused an ebb in Glyndebourne's spirits and confidence, with the company reverting to four productions in 1972, the highlight of which was Peter Hall's staging of Monteverdi's *Il ritorno d'Ulisse in patria*, conducted by Leppard, designed by John Bury, with Janet Baker and Benjamin Luxon in the lead roles. The gods and goddesses were largely airborne, suspended from a huge grid which moved them on both vertical and horizontal planes and which caused the production to be accorded the soubriquet 'Monteverdi's Flying Circus' from Anne Howells, who sang the role of the goddess Minerva.

1972 also sowed another seed which was to flourish in succeeding years, namely the engagement of Bernard Haitink to conduct *Die Entführung*.

This was also the year that Southern Television started its long association with Glyndebourne – an association which lasted productively until they lost their franchise in 1982. The library of Glyndebourne recordings made by Southern, combined with those which had been made by the BBC, represented a formidable body of work accessible to a widespread audience.

1973 saw the consolidation of Glyndebourne's partnerships, with Hall and Bury on the one part and Cox on the other – partnerships which were to bear a lot of fruit over the years.

Hall directed *Figaro* in a definitive production with Pritchard conducting, and the three leading ladies consisting of Cotrubas, Frederica von Stade, and Kiri Te Kanawa sharing with Elizabeth Harwood. In 1977 Hall and Bury went on to stage *Don Giovanni*, with Pritchard and Haitink sharing honours in the pit, and in 1978 *Così* with Haitink and Maria Ewing (later Mrs Hall) as Dorabella. These three productions brought a new depth of understanding to the Mozart/da Ponte operas and recaptured Glyndebourne's position internationally at front of stage in this pivotal area of the operatic repertoire.

1975 **1976** **1977** **1978** **1979**

1975: *The Rake's Progress* with David Hockney's first designs for opera

1978: Bernard Haitink succeeded John Pritchard as Music Director

Cox staged Strauss's *Capriccio* in the old but unageing set created by Lennon ten years before – with Söderström again playing the Countess. He updated the action from its museum-like intended context of the 18th century to the 1920s, which caused me consternation. (Updating operas was considered heinous.) However, Cox's treatment of the opera, in decorations, furnishings and costumes designed by Martin Battersby, brought the piece vividly to life and caused it to remain in Glyndebourne's repertoire until 1998 – and to give it a life that extended worldwide.

Capriccio in 1973 also occasioned the engagement of Andrew Davis at the start of his career as Pritchard's back-up for a few performances. This was the beginning of a long association with Glyndebourne.

In 1974, Cox memorably staged Strauss's *Intermezzo* in designs by Martin Battersby with Söderström playing the role of Strauss's wife in this autobiographical piece. This production deservedly won the Evening Standard Award. I think it fair to claim that these two productions placed Strauss's comedies firmly on the international map.

Just as Ebert and Busch had brought new life to the Mozart operas and Gui to the Rossini comedies, so Leppard had done to the early Italian Baroque repertoire and now Peter Hall was again doing to the Mozart/da Ponte operas and John Cox to the Strauss comedies. These were the arteries which gave life-blood to the body of repertory in Glyndebourne's first four decades and gave the Festival and its touring branch a sense of purpose and direction – supplemented of course by a wide variety of other operas.

From 1973 on, there were, of course, ups and downs in the programme planning. Gottfried von Einem's *The Visit of the Old Lady* that year was an aberration. On the other hand, Jonathan Miller's staging of *The Cunning Little Vixen* in 1975 was enchanting and a harbinger – as things turned out – of Glyndebourne's courtship with Janáček in the 1980s and 1990s. The crowning triumph of 1975 was, however, John Cox's production of Stravinsky's *The Rake's Progress*, in David Hockney's designs with Haitink conducting – what a line-up of talent ...

The following year also provided a see-saw of artistic fortune. Verdi's *Falstaff*, with Donald Gramm in the title role (he had scored a huge success the previous year as Nick Shadow in *The Rake*), was directed and designed unsurpassably (in my experience) by Jean-Pierre Ponnelle whose imagination, invention and theatrical skills knew no bounds. *Pelléas et Mélisande*, on the other hand, in my opinion gloomily directed by René Terrasson, had best be forgotten. Poor Haitink found himself the sacrificial lamb on the altar of the theatrical cock-up which Debussy's masterpiece was subjected to, while Pritchard basked in the glory of (and contributed constructively to) the success of the performance of Verdi's masterpiece.

In addition to Hall's staging of *Don Giovanni* in 1977, a new production of Strauss's dramatically intractable opera *Die schweigsame Frau* was directed by Cox and conducted by Davis; but it was Felicity Lott's debut at Glyndebourne in the role of Anne Trulove (in *The Rake*) and Simon Rattle's debut conducting the revival of *The Vixen* which stick in the memory. Rattle was 21 at the time and fresh out of the Royal Academy, where I heard him in a student performance of Offenbach's *La jolie parfumeuse*. I recommended him to the music staff in 1974 and he was engaged by the department for the next two years, albeit with the stumbling block that his piano-playing took second place to his skills as a percussionist. Over 26 years Rattle conducted 15 productions for Glyndebourne (including GTO).

1977 saw the curtain come down on Pritchard's career at Glyndebourne – a career which started in 1947 on the music staff, from which he graduated to Chorus Master in 1949, and Busch's back-up conductor in 1951, whence he became the fully-fledged conductor of *Idomeneo* in 1952. From that year until and including the 1977 Festival he conducted every year at Glyndebourne, covering an impressive array of operas. He was a conductor with a phenomenally quick grasp of a huge range of repertoire. This God-given facility contributed to his sybaritic lifestyle. His schedule was professionally and internationally stretched, but he was able to enjoy the good things in life. On his day his performance was unbeatable, but he had his days of free-wheeling. My regret is that he was never signed up by a recording company. This would, in my view, have given him the extended exposure which would have won him widespread recognition for a place among the foremost conductors of the second half of the 20th century. He certainly had that recognition from within the profession. He was a mainstay in Glyndebourne's history.

Additional to Hall's production of *Così* in 1978, a staging which like his other two Mozart/da Ponte operas went to the heart of these operas, Cox and Hockney staged *Die Zauberflöte*, with Haitink conducting, a production which inevitably caused a lot of media hype and triumphantly caught the public's imagination. This was the first production Haitink conducted as Glyndebourne's new Music Director. He had succeeded Pritchard as principal conductor of the LPO and was again taking over his baton at Glyndebourne – a logical progression given that the LPO was (and, come to that, still is) Glyndebourne's resident orchestra. Haitink's tenure as Music Director lasted ten halcyon years …

In the final year of the decade, Hall directed a wholly convincing new production of *Fidelio*, conducted by Haitink, and with Söderström singing Leonore. She may not have had the vocal guns to sing this part in a larger theatre, but in the intimacy of the old theatre at Glyndebourne she brought a poignant sense of realism to this most heroically sensitive of roles. Cox that year staged a production of Glyndebourne's only foray into the field of Haydn's operas, *La fedeltà premiata*, with Haitink conducting. Haydn's operatic comedies seem to be based dramatically on an invariable formula which, if pursued, leads to a dead end. At the start of her career, Kathy Battle made her only appearance at Glyndebourne in *La fedeltà* and woke the audience up …

1979 also saw a revival of *Ulisse*, with von Stade and Stilwell as a glamorous and moving pair of reunited protagonists in this most heroic of tales.

The 1970s were a turning point in Glyndebourne's financial welfare. Early in the decade I came to know a gentleman by the name of Alex Alexander, a Czech by birth. In the 1950s my father had had the good fortune to meet up with Miki Sekers – a Hungarian by birth who helped Glyndebourne retain its financial self-sufficiency; and I was blessed by my encounter and friendship with Alexander who simply put sponsorship onto a plane not envisaged by the Glyndebourne executive at the time. I invited him to join the Glyndebourne Arts Trust in 1975 and then onto the executive Board of Glyndebourne Productions Limited in 1979. He not only transformed the company's finances, but significantly helped to reconfigure the executive's administrative and financial philosophy. He was an indispensable part of Glyndebourne's growth and development in the 1970s and 1980s and his legacy remains a forceful component in the company's financial structure and operations.

With this financial stabilisation …

Views of the gardens, 1970 (ZOË DOMINIC)

0775 -42
-22
-43
-40
-44
-41
KODAK
SAFETY FILM

La Calisto rehearsals, 1970.

RIGHT: Federico Davià, Peter Hall and James Bowman (ANTHONY CRICKMAY)

BOTTOM: Hugues Cuénod, Peter Hall and Janet Hughes (ANTHONY CRICKMAY)

OPPOSITE: Hugues Cuénod rehearsing his role as Linfea (ANTHONY CRICKMAY)

The Rake's Progress, 1975.

TOP: Set model showing. Moran Caplat, Annabelle Hawtrey (Props Manager), Stephen Jetten (Harkers Studio scenery painter), June Dandridge (Production Manager), designer David Hockney and director John Cox (Director of Productions) (GUY GRAVETT)

ABOVE: Hockney painting the scenery (DONALD COOPER)

OPPOSITE TOP: Jill Gomez as Anne Trulove and Leo Goeke as Tom Rakewell in rehearsal (GUY GRAVETT)

OPPOSITE BOTTOM LEFT: David Hockney and John Cox discussing the production (GUY GRAVETT)

OPPOSITE BOTTOM RIGHT: Bernard Haitink, John Cox and David Hockney during rehearsal (GUY GRAVETT)

The Cunning Little Vixen rehearsals in the Ebert Room, 1975.

ABOVE LEFT: Conductor Raymond Leppard with director Jonathan Miller and repetiteur Stuart Bedford (GUY GRAVETT)

LEFT: Jonathan Miller (GUY GRAVETT)

RIGHT: Raymond Leppard and Jonathan Miller rehearsing the girls from Malling Primary School (GUY GRAVETT)

CENTRE: Norma Burrowes as the Vixen with her Fox Cubs, 1977 (CHRIS CORMACK)

BOTTOM: Louise Christie as a Fox Cub, 1977 (CHRIS CORMACK)

Il ritorno d'Ulisse in patria, 1972.

ABOVE: Janet Baker and Benjamin Luxon as Penelope and Ulisse, finally reunited at the end of the opera (GUY GRAVETT)

OPPOSITE TOP: Conductor Raymond Leppard and director Peter Hall in rehearsal (GUY GRAVETT)

OPPOSITE CENTRE: Jonathan Hinden, John Wakefield, Peter Hall, Brian Dickie, Ian Caley and Benjamin Luxon at an archery rehearsal (GUY GRAVETT)

OPPOSITE BOTTOM: Benjamin Luxon drawing Ulisse's mighty bow (GUY GRAVETT)

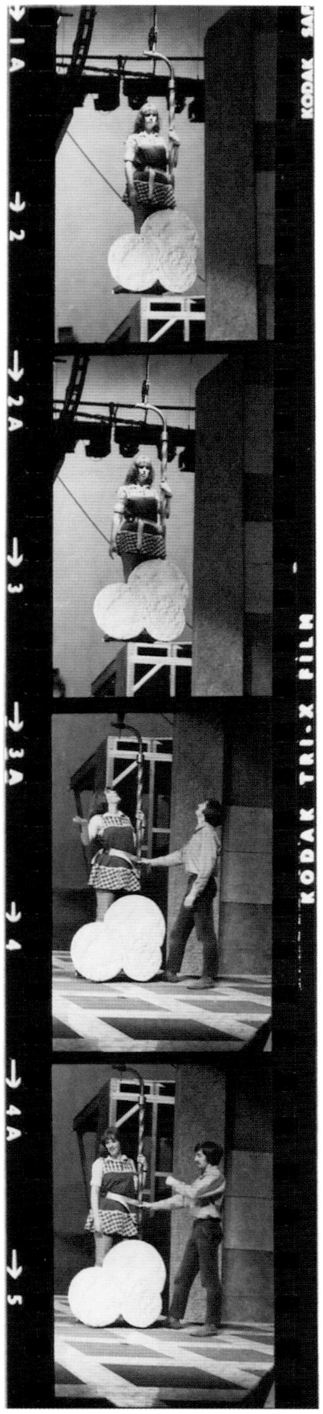

'Monteverdi's Flying Circus', 1972.

ABOVE AND RIGHT: Anne Howells as Minerva and Benjamin Luxon as Ulisse (GUY GRAVETT)

OPPOSITE TOP: Robert Lloyd (Neptune) and David Hughes (Jove) (GUY GRAVETT)

OPPOSITE BOTTOM LEFT: Robert Lloyd (Neptune) (GUY GRAVETT)

OPPOSITE BOTTOM RIGHT: Designer John Bury (GUY GRAVETT)

La Calisto, directed by Peter Hall and designed by John Bury, 1970.

ABOVE: James Bowman as Endimione and Janet Baker as Diana (ZOË DOMINIC)

OPPOSITE: The three goddesses in the Prologue, Nature, Eternity and Destiny (ZOË DOMINIC)

Falstaff, directed and designed by Jean-Pierre Ponnelle, 1976.
TOP: Max-René Cosotti as Fenton and Elizabeth Gale as Nannetta (GUY GRAVETT)
CENTRE: Elizabeth Gale (Nannetta), Kay Griffel (Alice), Reni Penkova (Meg) and Nucci Condò (Mistress Quickly) (GUY GRAVETT)
BOTTOM: Donald Gramm (Falstaff) and Nucci Condò (Mistress Quickly) (GUY GRAVETT)

OPPOSITE: Paolo Montarsolo as Selim and Graziella Sciutti as Fiorilla during a break in rehearsals of *Il turco in Italia*, 1970 (ZOË DOMINIC)

Glyndebourne's first commissioned opera, *The Rising of the Moon*, 1970. Composed by Nicholas Maw, to a libretto by Beverley Cross, conducted by Raymond Leppard, and directed by Colin Graham with designs by Osbert Lancaster.

LEFT: Raymond Leppard and Colin Graham at rehearsal (GUY GRAVETT)

BELOW: Nicholas Maw with Osbert Lancaster and Colin Graham examining the props on set (ZOË DOMINIC)

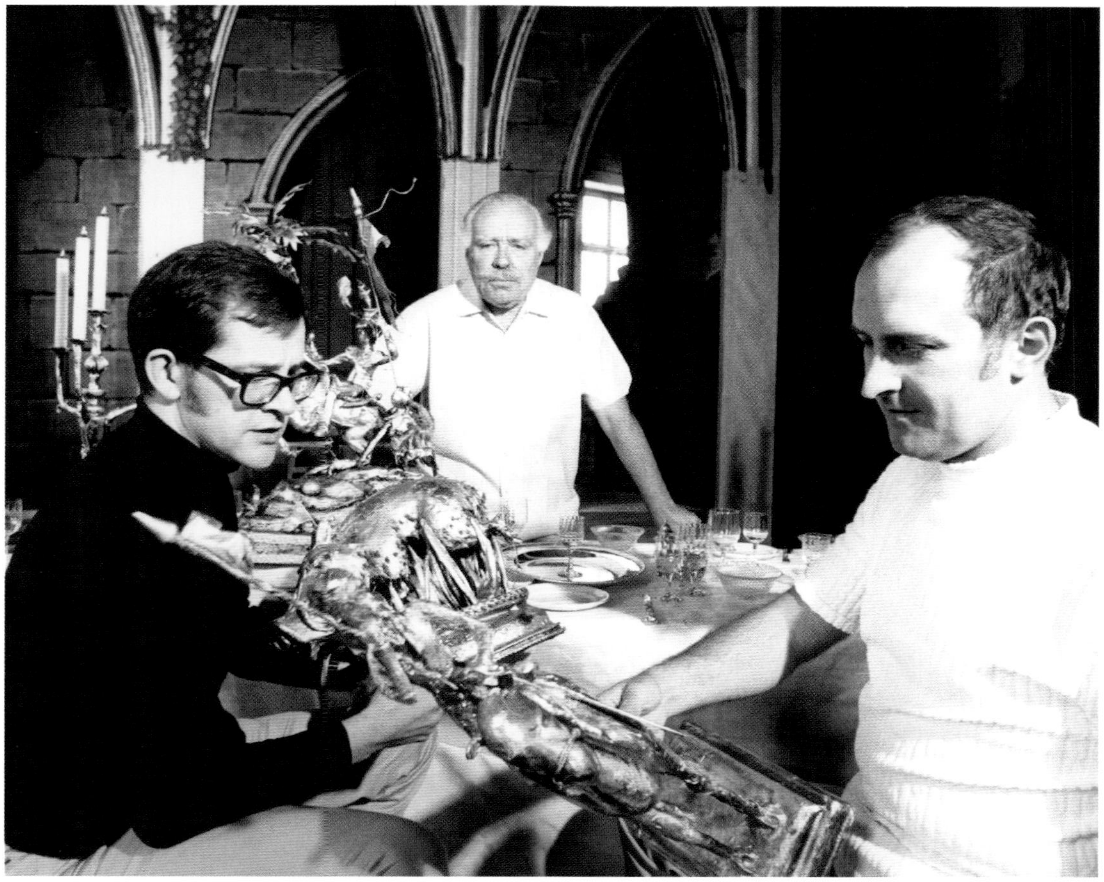

RIGHT: John Fryatt as Captain Lillywhite and Richard Van Allan as Colonel Lord Jowler (GUY GRAVETT)
BELOW: Anne Howells as Cathleen Sweeney with John Wakefield as Cornet John Stephen Beaumont (GUY GRAVETT)

ABOVE: Elisabeth Söderström as Christine, *Intermezzo*, 1974 (GUY GRAVETT)

OPPOSITE: Felicity Lott making her Glyndebourne Touring Opera debut as the Countess in *Capriccio*, 1976 (GUY GRAVETT)

Nature As Thy Teacher

Leave all love and hope behind
out of sight is out of mind

The Rake's Progress, directed by John Cox and designed by David Hockney, 1975.

ABOVE LEFT: Tom's morning room with Donald Gramm as Nick Shadow and Leo Goeke as Tom Rakewell (GUY GRAVETT)

ABOVE RIGHT: Final curtain, Don Garrard (Trulove), Jill Gomez (Anne Trulove), Leo Goeke (Tom Rakewell), Rosalind Elias (Baba the Turk) and Donald Gramm (Nick Shadow) (GUY GRAVETT)

OPPOSITE TOP LEFT: Don Garrard (Trulove), Jill Gomez (Anne Trulove), Leo Goeke (Tom Rakewell) and Donald Gramm (Nick Shadow) (DONALD COOPER)

OPPOSITE TOP RIGHT: The brothel scene (DONALD COOPER)

OPPOSITE BOTTOM: Bedlam with Leo Goeke as Tom Rakewell (DONALD COOPER)

Peter Hall's double-cast production of Mozart's *Don Giovanni*, designed by John Bury, 1977.

TOP: Thomas Allen in the title role with Richard Van Allan as Leporello (PHILIP INGRAM)

RIGHT: Benjamin Luxon as Don Giovanni descending to hell (PHILIP INGRAM)

OPPOSITE: *Così fan tutte*, 1978. Maria Ewing as Dorabella and Håkan Hagegård as Guglielmo (GUY GRAVETT)

Le nozze di Figaro, the first of the three da Ponte operas directed by Peter Hall and designed by John Bury.

TOP: Frederica von Stade (Cherubino) with Ileana Cotrubas (Susanna), 1973 (GUY GRAVETT)

ABOVE: Ileana Cotrubas (Susanna) with Elizabeth Harwood (Countess), 1973 (GUY GRAVETT)

TOP RIGHT: Kiri Te Kanawa (Countess) and Benjamin Luxon (Count), 1973 (GUY GRAVETT)

CENTRE RIGHT: Kiri Te Kanawa as the Countess, 1974 (GUY GRAVETT)

ABOVE RIGHT: Elizabeth Gale (Susanna) and Thomas Allen (Figaro), 1974 (GUY GRAVETT)

ABOVE: *Die Zauberflöte*, directed by John Cox and designed by David Hockney with Benjamin Luxon (Papageno) and Felicity Lott (Pamina), 1978 (GUY GRAVETT)

ABOVE: Frederica von Stade as Penelope in the revival of *Il ritorno d'Ulisse in patria*, 1979 (GUY GRAVETT)

OPPOSITE: Jani Strasser in his office, 1972. Originally Audrey Mildmay's singing teacher in Vienna, he came to Glyndebourne in 1934 and devoted himself to the company as Head of Music staff and casting director until his retirement in 1972 (GUY GRAVETT)

Views of the gardens, 1970 (ZOÉ DOMINIC)

1980s

... the 1980s looked set fair. In the course of this decade, two strands of repertoire emerged and stand out in sharp relief. Britten's operas were embraced with passion after some 30-odd years of *froideur* between Glyndebourne and Aldeburgh, and Janáček's operas were given a profoundly distinctive dramatic and visual focus by the director Nikolaus Lehnhoff and his designer Tobias Hoheisel. It was these two strands which injected life-blood into Glyndebourne's continuing search for artistic direction.

The 1980 Festival opened with a new production of *Entführung*, conducted by Gustav Kuhn and directed by Peter Wood (inexplicably his only production at Glyndebourne) in designs of ravishing beauty by William Dudley with Willard White as Osmin and Gösta Winbergh (sadly his only appearance at Glyndebourne) as Belmonte.

The other new production that year, *Rosenkavalier*, conducted by Haitink and directed by Cox, was quirkish. Erté was a fascinating choice of designer for the piece, but caused more critical opprobrium than encomium, both of which were vented with fervour against or for the inescapable trademark of his style in the designs for the sets and costumes.

The following year saw the first Britten production since 1947, namely *A Midsummer Night's Dream* (championed and) conducted by Haitink, directed by Hall and designed definitively by Bury, with Ileana Cotrubas and James Bowman as rulers of the 'fairy kingdom'. The opening of the opera, in which the forest awakens and becomes enlivened – a recurrent characteristic in the production – until the sun sets

1980
Performances of *The Rake's Progress* in Paris

1981
Glyndebourne's first Britten opera since 1947 – new production of *A Midsummer*

1982
Brian Dickie succeeded Moran Caplat as General Administrator

1983

1984
Glyndebourne's 50th anniversary

Peter Hall made Artistic Director

just before the denouement, was magical. It is a production which possesses immortality – even now, some 28 years on, it continues to be held in stock. Peter Pears came out at the end of the first performance and simply said, 'I just wish Ben [Benjamin Britten] had been here tonight ... '

The other new production in 1981 was Rossini's *Barbiere*, directed by John Cox, with Maria Ewing as Rosina and Claudio Desderi as Bartolo, the start of a fruitful relationship with this intelligent 'stage animal'. In the 1982 revival the part of Almaviva was taken by Robert Gambill, who assumed the role of Tristan 22 years later – talk about a quantum leap ...

At the end of the 1981 Festival, Moran Caplat retired from his position as General Administrator after 33 years at the helm (he was a sailor in the Second World War and in any spare summer hours thereafter). Rudi Bing had been the General Manager from 1936 until 1948. So between the two of them they held sway for 45 years – a huge period in today's context. Caplat's period of greatest strength stands out most memorably during the years following my mother's death in 1953 and my father's widowerhood and waning powers – the 'Gui years' – until the mid-1960s when a lack of inspirational artistic leadership set in. During those post-war days he set the Good Ship Glyndebourne on a course which survived the choppy waters in the latter half of the 1960s.

So, in 1982, Brian Dickie (Caplat's second-in-command) took over as General Administrator and Anthony Whitworth-Jones took over Dickie's job as Administrator of GTO. It was a seemingly incestuous chain of events but, I'd like to think, testimony to Glyndebourne's trust and faith in the logical progression of its in-house executive talent, testimony borne out by the next seven years, during which Dickie reigned supreme, and then Whitworth-Jones up to 1998.

That year, Prokofiev's *Love for Three Oranges*, staged in a new production by Frank Corsaro, in designs by Maurice Sendak and conducted by Haitink, proved to be a triumph of comic and creative inconsequentiality. The most consequential aspect of this brief foray into the territory of Prokofiev was the tie-up between the sponsor – Cointreau – and the name of the opera. It is a work which, also for no consequential reason, I hold dear to my heart – a delicious fairy-tale concoction.

The other new production that year was Gluck's *Orfeo ed Euridice*, conducted by Leppard and directed by Hall. This production was memorable for Janet Baker's performance as Orfeo. Ferrier did her first Orfeo at Glyndebourne, and 35 years later Dame Janet did her last Orfeo there – indeed, it was the last operatic performance of her career – a truly great artist.

The 1983 Festival delivered a new production of *Idomeneo*, conducted by Haitink and directed by Trevor Nunn (making his debut at Glyndebourne), with Philip Langridge and Carol Vaness giving definitive performances of the title role and Electra respectively; and a new production of *Cenerentola* remembered chiefly for Desderi's performance of Don Magnifico, and a newcomer, Alessandro Corbelli, in the role of Dandini. Among the revivals, *Intermezzo* featured Felicity Lott as an unsurpassable Christine, a role which, until then, had been the exclusive preserve of Elisabeth Söderström.

The following year we celebrated Glyndebourne's 50th birthday, to which Her Majesty the Queen was invited to a performance. She asked what the Festival's programme held in store, and I replied, 'Well, *Figaro* perhaps?' to which she countered with her celebrated and very perceptive comment, 'Is that the piece in which somebody loses a pin?' In the event she came to the new production of Strauss's *Arabella*, conducted by Haitink and directed by Cox, with Andrew Davis's future wife, Gianna Rolandi, making her debut at Glyndebourne in the role of Zdenka.

The other new production in 1984 was *Poppea* in a revised version (or perversion, as the purists preferred to view it) of Leppard's 1962 edition. It was conducted of course by Leppard and directed by Hall, with Ewing (his wife) in the title role.

This was the year that Peter Hall, still the Director of the National Theatre, was appointed Artistic Director of

1985

1986

Porgy and Bess, the first British production in the UK

Visit to the Hong Kong Arts Festival

Establishment of the education department

1987

GTO world premiere of *The Electrification of the Soviet Union*

1988

Beginning of Nikolaus Lehnhoff's Janáček cycle

1989

Anthony Whitworth-Jones took over as General Director

Andrew Davis became Glyndebourne's fifth Music Director

Glyndebourne, having directed by then some 18 productions over 14 years with virtually unvarying success in the Festival.

In January 1984 Glyndebourne staged at the National Theatre the almost completed score of *Where the Wild Things Are,* commissioned from Oliver Knussen and the writer of the book on which the piece is based, Maurice Sendak. This piece was then paired on Glyndebourne's autumn tour with *Higglety, Pigglety Pop!* commissioned from the same creative team, the double bill being directed by Corsaro in, of course, designs by Sendak. Knussen, however, failed again to complete the score of this second piece, despite urgent pressure from Glyndebourne and constant reassurances from him, leaving a crucial central section of the score un-composed. With less than a week before the first performance, I contacted an old friend, Bamber Gascoigne, and asked him to help bail us out of this impasse by scripting a spoken connection between the composed sections and, more time-consumingly, taking on the job of performing this spatchcocked link over some six weeks. He dropped all engagements and came to our rescue. To fail to provide to the commissioning agent one completed score and to do this again to far greater injurious degree in the case of its companion piece is, in my opinion, professional incompetence. In 1985 this double bill was mounted in the Festival in its 'completed' state.

The pattern of staging five productions in the Festival each year had remained more or less constant since 1970, but in 1985, reflecting the strength of audience demand and the UK economy, the programme was extended to six – a pattern which has continued almost unchanged ever since.

The first new production in 1985 was *Carmen*, with Haitink and Hall, and with Ewing in the title role. The other was *Albert Herring*, with Hall directing and John Gunter designing an immortal production, with Haitink conducting and John Graham-Hall definitively in the title role, with Alan Opie as a laddish Sid, both of whom some 23 years later, found themselves performing the more mature roles of the Mayor and the Vicar in that very same production at Glyndebourne.

The highlight in 1986 was of course *Porgy and Bess*, with Willard White and Cynthia Haymon in the title roles. It was a production by Trevor Nunn, in designs by John Gunter, and conducted by Simon Rattle. It was Brian Dickie's brainchild. *Porgy* was an idiosyncratic beacon in Glyndebourne's annals – idiosyncratic in the sense that you would have expected some major enterprising company to have given it long ago the full operatic treatment which Gershwin craved for when he wrote it. We simply set out to affirm this work as an operatic masterpiece, and I believe we came out well from this endeavour. (Incidentally we received that year a questionnaire from the Arts Council relating to racial equality on our payroll!)

The other new production – a mixed success – in 1986 was *Simon Boccanegra*, directed by Hall in designs by Gunter (14th-century Genoa reflected by its Mediterranean bay in the first scene of Act 1 was one of the most beautiful sets I have

seen on any stage), and conducted by Haitink, with Carol Vaness a magnetic force as Amelia (she sang Donna Anna equally hypnotically in *Don Giovanni* that year).

In 1987 I mentioned in my foreword to the programme book the idea of rebuilding the theatre as 'a glint in my eye'. The idea was prompted by the need to respond to audience demand for tickets, the need to provide a cogently designed building in place of the piecemeal structure which had materialised over half a century, and the need to create a stable base for the next half century, and more. At that time I gave us six years: three in which to think about this and cultivate a constructive response to the idea, and three in which to raise the money and carry out the construction work.

This year Glyndebourne dipped its toe again into the Verdi repertoire with a new production of *Traviata* and the familiar team of Haitink, Hall and Gunter with Marie McLaughlin as Violetta. Ravel's double bill of *L'Heure espagnole* and *L'Enfant et les sortilèges* was the other new production in 1987, with Rattle, Corsaro and Sendak – not a patch on their team effort in *Love for Three Oranges*.

Particular mention has to be made here of Hugues Cuénod's farewell performance at Glyndebourne. In 1987, at the age of 85, he performed the role of M. Taupe (the Prompter) in *Capriccio*, having appeared in every season except one since 1954. Mind you, a year or so later he made his debut at the Met in New York as the Emperor in *Turandot*. And now at the time of writing he is 106.

In my foreword to the 1988 programme book I expressed conciliatory tones to those concerned about the growing prospect of the rebuild of the theatre, highlighting more than anything that the risks of such a major re-development going wrong would – given the centrality of the family's heart-beat in Glyndebourne – rebound and have greater repercussions against Mary and me than against them.

The new productions this year were a mixed bag. *Kát'a Kabanová* – with supertitles. The Royal Opera House had introduced them in performances for schoolchildren, but Glyndebourne pioneered them for general consumption by adult audiences. Artistically, it was the introduction of Nikolaus Lehnhoff (Brian Dickie's choice) and Tobias Hoheisel as director and designer of *Kát'a*, which grabbed the headlines, and which continued to do so with their re-conception of Janáček's operas at Glyndebourne over the next few years.

In 1988, *Falstaff*, with Haitink and Hall, came back in its third incarnation at Glyndebourne with Desderi in the title role. But it was *The Electrification of the Soviet Union*, an opera based on Pasternak's *The Last Summer*, commissioned by Glyndebourne from the composer Nigel Osborne and poet Craig Raine, in collaboration with the director Peter Sellars, which got the press – and audiences – into a state of confused excitement. It was a challenging work in every aspect and made no concession to be otherwise. It was a work created in 1987 for GTO, thus reinforcing a trend whereby GTO became a production company for the purpose of helping to broaden the Festival's repertory output, particularly in the case of more experimental pieces. It therefore reversed GTO's previous role of being almost wholly dependent for its artistic diet on the Festival.

In 1989 it was all change. Firstly, Dickie departed after a triumphant period during which he broadened the development of Glyndebourne's artistic base, streamlined its administration and financial controls – and reinvented the catering department to clamorous joy. Whitworth-Jones, his number two, succeeded him. Secondly, Haitink took up the offer of music directorship at the Royal Opera House, having reigned supreme at Glyndebourne for ten invigorating years, and the baton was passed to Andrew Davis. Thirdly, Alex Alexander took his Midas touch to the Royal Opera House after 15 enriching years at Glyndebourne. And fourthly, the Orchestra of the Age of Enlightenment replaced the LPO for the first time for one production only (*Figaro*) – a turn of events much influenced on the one hand by Rattle, who championed this orchestra, and embraced on the other by Dickie, who foresaw the need to provide a platform for period instruments at Glyndebourne.

Jenůfa was the only new production given in 1989 with Davis conducting and Lehnhoff directing in Hoheisel's designs. This production, following the success of *Kát'a* in the previous year, combined, above all, with the chilling and in turns deeply moving performance of Anja Silja as the Kostelnička, set the seal well and truly on Glyndebourne's embrace of Janáček's works.

So with a number of quite major changes happening at Glyndebourne in the last year of this decade …

ABOVE: Looking through the Irish yews towards the croquet lawn and Urn Garden, 1984 (AF KERSTING)

OPPOSITE: The lake in summer (AF KERSTING)

The Electrification of the Soviet Union, 1987. A commission for Glyndebourne Touring Opera.

ABOVE: Rehearsals in the Ebert Room with composer Nigel Osborne, librettist Craig Raine and director Peter Sellars (GUY GRAVETT)

OPPOSITE: Full cast meeting in the Organ Room. Peter Sellars seated in the centre, Craig Raine, Nigel Osborne, George Christie, Mary Christie Anthony Whitworth-Jones, and, crouching, Dennis Marks of the BBC (GUY GRAVETT)

ABOVE AND OPPOSITE TOP: *Porgy and Bess* rehearsals in the Lily Davis Room, 1986 (GUY GRAVETT)

OPPOSITE BOTTOM: Willard White talking with director Trevor Nunn (GUY GRAVETT)

Albert Herring, directed by Peter Hall and designed by John Gunter, 1985.

TOP: John Graham-Hall (Albert) and Patricia Kern (Mrs Herring) (GUY GRAVETT)

CENTRE: Jean Rigby (Nancy), Alan Opie (Sid) and John Graham-Hall (Albert) (GUY GRAVETT)

RIGHT: Patricia Johnson (Lady Billows), Felicity Palmer (Florence Pike), Derek Hammond-Stroud (Mr Gedge), Elizabeth Gale (Miss Wordsworth) and Richard Van Allan (Superintendent Budd) (GUY GRAVETT)

A Midsummer Night's Dream, directed by Peter Hall and designed by John Bury, 1984.

OPPOSITE TOP: James Bowman (Oberon) and Elizabeth Gale (Tytania) (GUY GRAVETT)

OPPOSITE BOTTOM LEFT: Jamie Gates (Puck) and James Bowman (Oberon) (GUY GRAVETT)

OPPOSITE BOTTOM RIGHT: Curt Appelgren (Bottom) and Elizabeth Gale (Tytania) (GUY GRAVETT)

L'Amour des Trois Oranges, directed by Frank Corsaro and designed by Maurice Sendak, 1982 (GUY GRAVETT)

Porgy and Bess, directed by Trevor Nunn and designed by John Gunter, 1986.

ABOVE: Willard White (Porgy), 'O Lawd, I'm on my way' (GUY GRAVETT)

TOP RIGHT: Willard White (Porgy) and Cynthia Haymon (Bess) (GUY GRAVETT)

CENTRE RIGHT: Cynthia Haymon (Bess), Gregg Baker (Crown), Damon Evans (Sportin' Life), Bruce Hubbard (Jake) and Willard White (Porgy) (GUY GRAVETT)

RIGHT: Marietta Simpson (Maria) and Damon Evans (Sportin' Life) (GUY GRAVETT)

Kát'a Kabanová, directed by Nikolaus Lehnhoff and designed by Tobias Hoheisel, 1988.

OPPOSITE TOP: Louise Winter (Varvara), Nancy Gustafson (Kát'a), Ryland Davies (Tichon) and Felicity Palmer (the Kabanicha) (GUY GRAVETT)

OPPOSITE BOTTOM: The final scene with Felicity Palmer and Nancy Gustafson (GUY GRAVETT)

The Electrification of the Soviet Union, directed by Peter Sellars and designed by George Tsypin (sets) and Duná Ramicová (costumes), 1987.

TOP AND ABOVE: Elizabeth Laurence and Omar Ebrahim as Anna and Serezha (GUY GRAVETT)

OPPOSITE TOP: Jonathan Veira as Lemokh and Omar Ebrahim as Serezha (GUY GRAVETT)

OPPOSITE BOTTOM: Linda Hirst as Natasha with Omar Ebrahim as Serezha (GUY GRAVETT)

Where The Wild Things Are, directed by Frank Corsaro and designed by Maurice Sendak, 1984.

LEFT: George Christie and Anthony Whitworth-Jones (GUY GRAVETT)

BOTTOM LEFT: A Wild Thing meets some children at the National Theatre (GUY GRAVETT)

Education projects.

TOP: East Sussex and Kent Schools' Festival at Glyndebourne with Richard Stilgoe as compère on stage with *L'Heure espagnole*, 1987.

The first Schools' Festival took place in 1979 and it became a biennial event (GUY GRAVETT)

ABOVE: *Albert Herring* project at Glyndebourne with John Graham-Hall as Albert, 1986 (GUY GRAVETT)

ERTE

TOP: Official visit of the Queen in 1984 in celebration of Glyndebourne's 50th anniversary for a performance of *Arabella* (GUY GRAVETT)

ABOVE: George Christie, Moran Caplat and Brian Dickie (GUY GRAVETT)

OPPOSITE TOP: *Der Rosenkavalier* party, 1980. Christopher Bridge, George Christie, Donald Gramm, Erté, Mary Christie, Nucci Condò and Nicholas Snowman (GUY GRAVETT)

OPPOSITE BOTTOM: *Albert Herring* production meeting with Bernard Haitink, Brian Dickie, George Christie and Peter Hall, held in Peter Hall's office at the National Theatre, 1985 (ZOË DOMINIC)

Members of the audience, 1982

(JANE BOWN)

1990s

... the 1990s faced some new and stimulating repertory-based challenges. Some of these challenges were to a degree aimed at the audience and some were self-inflicted. They came in the form of commissioned operas from Michael Tippett, Harrison Birtwistle and Jonathan Dove, repertory rarities such as Rossini's *Ermione* and Britten's *Owen Wingrave*, together with Glyndebourne's increasing collaboration with the new wave of directors like Peter Sellars and Graham Vick.

Glyndebourne appeared intent on breaking new ground and its spirit of adventure was growing with the inevitable attendant consequence of increasing risk of failure in some areas of its output. However, one strand of its output which memorably emerged in this decade was the start of its dalliance with Handel.

The new productions in the first year of this decade cannot be accounted as successful. *The Magic Flute*, directed by Sellars and set on a Californian freeway, was roundly booed on the first night. Edward Heath was in the audience and accosted me at the end. About a minute into his assault, I beckoned Sellars over and introduced him as the director of the production. Mr Heath turned the full blast of his fire power on Sellars who, after 15 seconds, turned to me and said loudly, 'It's just like being attacked by a hot-water bottle.' Of the other production, Tippett's *New Year*, the libretto doomed it to failure.

The following year commemorated the bicentenary of Mozart's death with the performance of six of his operas. A new production of *Così* – directed with a depth of insight and sensitivity by Trevor Nunn, in designs by Maria Bjørnson,

1990	1991	1992	1993	1994
European premiere of		Last season in the old theatre	Glyndebourne at the South	Opening of the new opera house

set on an ocean liner in the 1920s, and conducted by Rattle – was a triumph with the audience, and almost totally with the critics – Amanda Roocroft (Fiordiligi) in particular scoring a successful debut at the Festival.

The other new production to Glyndebourne (and about time, too), was *La clemenza di Tito*, conducted by Davis and directed by Nicholas Hytner, making his first very welcome appearance on Glyndebourne's 'billboards'.

In the 1991 programme book I announced that the rebuild of the theatre was now poised to go ahead. Two-thirds of the funding target had been pledged, and the Boards of the Glyndebourne Arts Trust and Glyndebourne Productions Limited had given the project their blessing. Michael Hopkins's architectural designs had reached an advanced stage, the team of consultants who would organise the construction process was in place, planning permission had been granted, and a detailed programme had been laid down. It stretched from autumn 1991 to spring 1992 for the first phase of the re-development, and from August 1992 to spring 1994 for the major work in the second phase.

So, in 1992, a Festival was mounted between phases one and two, albeit with the loss of the gardens at the north of the theatre which had been deeply excavated for the new rehearsal stage and backstage areas of the building, which would turn the old theatre through 180 degrees on its axis. This excavated area was boarded off, with peepholes allowing the audience to get a grip of the reality of Glyndebourne's preparations for thrusting its survival into the next millennium. (The peepholes also encouraged the generation of financial support for the rebuild – the gleam in my eye having reached a convincing point of no return.)

The Festival in 1992 mounted two fine new productions: Britten's *Peter Grimes*, conducted by Davis and directed by Nunn with predictable perception; and Tchaikovsky's *The Queen of Spades*, again with our Music Director, Davis, and with the director Graham Vick making a victorious first appearance at Glyndebourne. His production was justly given the Evening Standard Award for Opera that year. Nancy Gustafson (at that time Mrs Brian Dickie) made her debut at Glyndebourne in the role of the ill-fated Lisa, Sergei Leiferkus did likewise in the role of Tomsky, and Felicity Palmer, an artist revered at Glyndebourne (and everywhere else) was unforgettable as the Countess.

A production of Britten's *Death in Venice*, new to the Festival but mounted on the previous year's Tour, was squeezed into the 1992 Festival, which ended on July 23rd, a month earlier than normal because of the pressure of the rebuild schedule. *Death in Venice*, conducted idiomatically and with affection by Graeme Jenkins, and directed by Stephen Lawless in sets and costumes by Hoheisel, provided star billing for Bob Tear in the central role of Aschenbach – of which he took full and fruitful advantage.

On July 24th, 1992, Glyndebourne mounted, in the presence of Prince Charles, its first and, to date, only gala performance. Generous sponsorship was provided, the conductors Davis and Haitink, and the singers – von Stade, Caballé, Raimondi, Lott, Luxon, Haymon and Kim Begley (standing in for Pavarotti who cancelled at the 11th hour) – together with the LPO and the Glyndebourne Chorus beneficently gave their services for free. Letheby and Christopher provided the catering for more than 1,000 people without charge, and various very munificent wine-growers donated oodles of their delicious liquid products. Janet Baker, Geraint Evans and Elisabeth Söderström made spoken tributes. The evening raised over £850,000.

And the following week the demolition gangs moved in, making very short shrift of the old building, which was the last purpose-built opera house to have been constructed in the UK until its reincarnation in 1994.

In the autumn of 1992, GTO found itself a waif without a base from which to operate for that year and the following. Sadler's Wells was the solution to our problem – a theatre even more derelict at that time than Glyndebourne and, like Glyndebourne, planning in the course of time its renascence and the total reconstruction of its much-beloved building.

Misper, first youth opera by

GTO world premiere of *Flight*

In 1993, Glyndebourne's first 'gap year' since the 1940s, a season of concerts was given in the Royal Festival Hall, consisting of three performances each of Berlioz's *Béatrice et Bénédict*, Beethoven's *Fidelio* and Lehár's *The Merry Widow*, with the LPO (of course) and a mixture of singers familiar to Glyndebourne and a smattering of star performers who for one reason or another were (or considered themselves to be) beyond our reach for engagement in the Festival. These concerts were Glyndebourne's token gesture to keep its Festival flag flying while it was homeless.

Glyndebourne's rebirth gestated for 20 months following demolition. For me this was an enthralling period. I held no regret about knocking down the old theatre, which was long past its sell-by date – the sight lines in the auditorium were poor, the acoustics were dry and unflattering, the leg-room was crippling, the wing-space on stage was a nightmare for designers, and the list went on. For years I had yearned to escape from the restrictions which, by virtue of the changes and extensions made over a long period to the old theatre, I had inherited. There was only one possible cure for these restrictions: a total rebuild. It was imperative if Glyndebourne was to be assured of a position whereby it could compete economically for survival and measure up to the artistic and technical demands of the 20th century.

In the late 1980s, the UK economy was buoyant, the political climate for private enterprise to take a bold step was propitious, and the demand for seats far exceeded our capacity to supply. By early 1992 we had raised 80 per cent of our £33m target without a penny from the public purse (or Lottery, which didn't exist then), thanks to the thriving market. What we hadn't anticipated was the good fortune which the 1991 recession then brought to us by way of reduced contract prices in the construction industry. Our timing on this project turned out to be providentially lucky.

One of our trustees, John Botts (later to become Chairman of the Glyndebourne Arts Trust), was a driving force in both the fund-raising and building programmes. Stuart Lipton of Stanhope Properties provided invaluable advice from the start of the planning process and lined up the team of consultants working with Michael and Patty Hopkins, the architects. It was a dream team which was wholly responsible for bringing the project in on budget and on time, for which Eric Gabriel, our Project Manager, together with Alan Lansdell, leading the Bovis Construction Management team, can be held particularly accountable.

Mention must also be made here of the major effect the rebuild had on an integral part of Glyndebourne, namely the layout of the gardens, its landscaping and the redisposition of buildings, over all of which my wife, Mary, together with Lady Mary Keen, took imaginative and creative control.

The end result in 1994 won every conceivable award (except one, where the new theatre at Glyndebourne was runner-up to a public lavatory in North London).

On March 28th, 1994 we had an acoustic test with the LPO, a line-up of distinguished soloists and the Glyndebourne Chorus performing under Haitink and Davis. I was asked why we troubled to stage this test with only two months to go before the opening night of the first Festival in the new theatre on May 28th. I replied that in so short a period there wasn't a hope of making any radical changes to satisfy subjective and suspect criticisms, but that it would give us satisfaction if the general consensus was favourable – such, I have to admit, was my confidence in Derek Sugden, the consultant acoustician.

The new theatre opened on May 28th with a performance of *Figaro* – the same date and opera as in 1934. Haitink conducting, Gerald Finley as Figaro and Renée Fleming (who had been Fiordiligi in the 1992 Festival) as the Countess are prominent in my memory. But the triumph in the season of the theatre's re-opening was *Eugene Onegin*, which, as I write this in the summer of 2008, remains as evergreen as ever. The other new production, *Don Giovanni*, with Rattle conducting, was controversial – not on account of Rattle, but because of Deborah Warner's, in my opinion, charmless direction.

The following year saw a new production of Rossini's rarely performed 'opera seria' *Ermione*, with Davis conducting and Vick bringing considerable inventive imagination to his presentation – and with Anna Caterina Antonacci and Bruce Ford as the gleaming stars in their testing roles as the protagonists.

Birtwistle's *The Second Mrs Kong*, commissioned by Glyndebourne and mounted on the 1994 tour by GTO, was the next novelty in the 1995 Festival. It was conducted by Elgar Howarth (with such facility as if it was a first exercise in Grade I piano) and both directed and designed unsurpassably by Tom Cairns, who replaced Richard Jones late in the planning process to allow the latter to take on the *Ring* cycle at the ROH.

And then came Janáček's *The Makropulos Case*, conducted by Davis and given a definitive production by Lehnhoff and Hoheisel, with Anja Silja as a riveting, almost indestructible, Emilia Marty, the central role. It was an unforgettably shattering experience in the theatre and sadly the last of the Lehnhoff/Hoheisel collaborations in the Janáček canon.

Theodora in 1996 was the start of Glyndebourne's dalliance with Handel, in which Bill Christie (no relation, but always known as 'Cousin Bill') made his debut in the Festival. Peter Sellars's updated production was as challenging as his 1990 *Flute*, although, unlike that production, this was a success, highlighting the risks inherent in 'concept' productions. Dawn Upshaw sang the role of Theodora beautifully but was, for me, counterfeit in contrast with Lorraine Hunt, who brought heart-rending pathos, both vocally and dramatically, to the role of Irene.

The three-act edition of Berg's *Lulu* – the other new production that year – was conducted by Davis, and was a rather hygienic, over-intellectualised take on this seediest of operas.

In 1997, Puccini's *Manon Lescaut*, with John Eliot Gardiner making, sadly, his only appearance in the pit at Glyndebourne, was given a somewhat minimalist production by Vick, while Rossini's *Le Comte Ory*, under Davis's baton, was staged with a welter of comic clichés by Jérôme Savary. Britten's *Owen Wingrave*, a production created in 1996 by GTO, was also staged in the 1997 Festival, and conducted by Ivor Bolton with Finley heading the cast. It's an interesting, but enigmatic piece in which Britten's obsession with pacifism is, for me, unsatisfactorily resolved at the end of the opera.

1998 saw the start of Vick's Mozart/da Ponte cycle. *Così* was staged in a production reminiscent of Marivaux's experimental theories dramatised for theatrical performance. This is perfectly workable for *Così*, a piece propounding experimental response as testified by its alternative title, *The School for Lovers*, but when Vick tried to embrace this concept later in his productions of *Figaro* and *Don Giovanni* it proved a step too far.

Rodelinda, under Bill Christie's beguiling baton, was then given in a new production staged by Jean-Marie Villégier, in designs by Nicolas de Lajartre and Pascale Cazales, with, in particular, Antonacci and Andreas Scholl holding the audience in thrall. The contrast between the productions of *Rodelinda* and *Theodora* was chasmic, but nonetheless victorious for both operas.

Simon Boccanegra, directed by Hall, was then brought back in totally new designs by Gunter. Despite the idiomatically excellent conducting of Mark Elder, it was not a success because of the inadequate casting of the central role of Boccanegra. Verdi baritones have always been in short supply. In the last 30 years they seem to have become an endangered species.

At the end of the 1998 Festival Anthony Whitworth-Jones gave up his position as General Director in which he had taken risks, treading that fine line between tradition and artistic success. There was a spirit of adventure in the air and this was his legacy. In his place, Nicholas Snowman was appointed to take over the reins of management, the fifth Chief Executive in Glyndebourne's 65 years.

The 1999 Festival opened with a strikingly beautiful and atmospheric production of Debussy's *Pelléas et Mélisande*, conducted by Davis and directed by Vick, in a single set designed by Paul Brown with a monumental and majestic spiral staircase, with which John Tomlinson (Golaud) vied for centre stage.

Smetana's *The Bartered Bride* was next, grippingly and lyrically conducted by Jiří Kout, and given in a new production by Lehnhoff and designed by Hoheisel. It thankfully avoided any kitsch which this *Volksoper* tends to be subjected to – but, instead, veered too much in the direction of mundaneness.

And thirdly, Jonathan Dove's *Flight*, commissioned by GTO for performance on tour in 1998, was staged under the baton of David Parry in an imaginative production by Richard Jones and designed by Giles Cadle. It is an opera which holds wide popular appeal, and has been embraced by opera houses internationally – and was brought back into Glyndebourne's repertory in the 2005 Festival. Dove is a composer with close ties to Glyndebourne, having worked productively with our very active and successful education department, particularly on three major projects involving a wide cross section of the communities of Hastings, Ashford and Peterborough.

At the end of 1999 I handed over my chairmanship to Gus, who had by then been on the Board of Glyndebourne Productions for ten years.

We were entering into a new millennium and, for Glyndebourne, a new era ...

ABOVE: Glyndebourne before the rebuild, 1991

OPPOSITE: Glyndebourne after the rebuild, 1996 (DAVID BOWIE)

ABOVE LEFT: *Così fan tutte*, directed by Trevor Nunn and designed by Maria Bjørnson, 1991. Suzanne Johnston (Dorabella), Gianna Rolandi (Despina), Kurt Streit (Ferrando), Claudio Desderi (Don Alfonso), Jake Gardiner (Guglielmo) and Amanda Roocroft (Fiordiligi) (GUY GRAVETT)

ABOVE RIGHT: *Peter Grimes*, directed by Trevor Nunn and designed by John Gunter, 1992. Alan Opie as Captain Balstrode with the Glyndebourne Chorus (GUY GRAVETT)

BELOW: *La clemenza di Tito*, directed by Nicholas Hytner and designed by David Fielding, 1991. Philip Langridge in the title role (GUY GRAVETT)

RIGHT: *Death in Venice*, directed by Stephen Lawless and designed by Tobias Hoheisel, 1992. Daniel Squire as Tadzio and Robert Tear as Aschenbach (GUY GRAVETT)

BELOW: Peter Sellars taking a full-cast rehearsal in the Ebert Room for *The Magic Flute*, 1990 (GUY GRAVETT)

TOP LEFT: Unchanged entrance to restaurants

TOP RIGHT: Red Foyer, stairs to Organ Room fireplace

ABOVE LEFT: Covered Way with box office to the left, shop centre and switchboard to the right

ABOVE RIGHT: Audrey Mildmay's dressing room (now used by Music Director Vladimir Jurowski)

RIGHT: Rehearsal space named the Lily Davis Room

OPPOSITE TOP: George Christie and architect Michael Hopkins looking through the back of the new auditorium model (JOEL HOPKINS)

OPPOSITE BOTTOM: Audience looking through the peepholes at the early building works, 1992 (JOEL HOPKINS)

ABOVE LEFT: George Christie at the controls of a digger, demolishing part of the old building, 1992 (GUS CHRISTIE)

ABOVE RIGHT: Auditorium during demolition looking towards the stage, 1992 (RICHARD DAVIES)

OPPOSITE: Looking out through the proscenium arch at the demolition work, 1992 (JOEL HOPKINS)

WIMPEY
WASTE

TOP, CENTRE, LEFT: Scaffolding studies (Top, GUS CHRISTIE; centre and left, RICHARD DAVIES)

OPPOSITE: The new theatre takes shape behind the house (GUS CHRISTIE)

First night in the new theatre, May 28th, 1994.

ABOVE: Celebratory fireworks seen from the hill above the car park (TOM REEVES)

OPPOSITE TOP: Peter Hall, Louise Flind and Roy Henderson – Glyndebourne's first Count in *Le nozze di Figaro*, 1934 (RICHARD DAVIES)

OPPOSITE BOTTOM: Curtain call for *Le nozze di Figaro* (RICHARD DAVIES)

Pelléas et Mélisande, directed by Graham Vick and designed by Paul Brown, 1999

TOP: Boxes of chrysanthemums in the rehearsal stage. Each of the 16,000 flowers was individually dyed by hand in the Glyndebourne props department. They were then inserted into the transparent floor sections to provide the carpet effect (MIKE HOBAN)

BELOW: Christian Tréguier (Arkel), Christiane Oelze (Mélisande) and John Tomlinson (Golaud), 2004 (MIKE HOBAN)

OPPOSITE: Constructing the staircase on stage. At the time the largest free-standing spiral staircase ever created for a stage work (MIKE HOBAN)

TOP AND ABOVE: *Ermione*, directed by Graham Vick and designed by Richard Hudson, 1996 (MIKE HOBAN)

TOP: *Lulu*, directed by Graham Vick and designed by Paul Brown, 1996 (MIKE HOBAN)

ABOVE: *The Makropulos Case*, directed by Nikolaus Lehnhoff and designed by Tobias Hoheisel, 1995 (MIKE HOBAN)

The Queen of Spades, directed by Graham Vick and designed by Richard Hudson, 1995.

ABOVE: Yuri Marusin as Herman (MIKE HOBAN)

OPPOSITE: Felicity Palmer as the Countess (MIKE HOBAN)

TOP: Conductor William Christie and director Peter Sellars during *Theodora* rehearsals, 1996 (MIKE HOBAN)

CENTRE: Chorus Master Christopher Moulds and conductor John Eliot Gardiner during rehearsals for *Manon Lescaut*, 1998 (MIKE HOBAN)

RIGHT: Conductor Mark Elder and director Peter Hall during rehearsals for *Simon Boccanegra*, 1998 (MIKE HOBAN)

OPPOSITE: Christopher Cowell (assistant director), Matthew Richardson (lighting designer), Graham Vick (Director of Productions), Andrew Davis (Music Director) in rehearsals for *Lulu*. Humphrey Burton of the BBC is in the background, 1996 (MIKE HOBAN)

TOP: Anja Silja as Emilia Marty, *The Makropulos Case*, 1995 (MIKE HOBAN)

ABOVE: Christine Schäfer as Lulu, 1996 (MIKE HOBAN)

TOP: Anna Caterina Antonacci as Rodelinda, 1998 (MIKE HOBAN)

ABOVE: Dawn Upshaw as Theodora, 1996 (MIKE HOBAN)

TOP: Kurt Streit, Umberto Chiummo, Andreas Scholl and Anna Caterina Antonacci during rehearsals for *Rodelinda* in the Ebert Room, 1998 (MIKE HOBAN)

ABOVE: Andreas Scholl in discussion with director Jean-Marie Villégier (MIKE HOBAN)

OPPOSITE: Andreas Scholl as Bertarido and Anna Caterina Antonacci as Rodelinda in the duet 'Io t'abbraccio' (MIKE HOBAN)

ABOVE: *Eugene Onegin*, directed by Graham Vick and designed by Richard Hudson, 1996. Elena Prokina as Tatyana and Wojtek Drabowicz in the title role (MIKE HOBAN)

OPPOSITE TOP: Peter Sellars rehearsing *Theodora* with Dawn Upshaw, David Daniels and Richard Croft, 1996 (MIKE HOBAN)

OPPOSITE CENTRE: Lorraine Hunt (Irene), and David Daniels (Didymus) (MIKE HOBAN)

Glyndebourne Education.

TOP AND BOTTOM: Director John Ramster takes an Opera Opportunity workshop. Opera Opportunity was set up in 1989 and thrives to this day with over 40,000 children having taken part since its inception (MIKE HOBAN)

OPPOSITE TOP: The third community opera, *In Search of Angels*, in Peterborough. The angels are seen descending the escalators in the shopping centre, 1995 (RICHARD DAVIES)

OPPOSITE BOTTOM: *Misper*, the education department's first full-scale youth opera, involving 75 children and six professional singers, was given in four performances on the Glyndebourne stage in March, 1997. Its huge success led to the formation of the Glyndebourne Youth Opera Groups, and a second youth opera, *Zoë*, followed two years later. This was subsequently made into a film by Channel 4 (MIKE HOBAN)

長城
歷史

YAMAH

GlyndebourneTouring Opera.

ABOVE RIGHT: Helen Field as Pearl with Deborah York as the Mirror in the premiere of *The Second Mrs Kong*, directed and designed by Tom Cairns, 1994 (MIKE HOBAN)

ABOVE: Conductor Ivor Bolton rehearsing William Dazeley in the title role of *Owen Wingrave*, with repetiteur Steven Naylor at the piano, 1995 (MIKE HOBAN)

LEFT: *Flight*, a new commission for 1998.

General Director Anthony Whitworth-Jones talking with composer Jonathan Dove.

Assistant conductor Christopher Moulds, repetiteur Stephen Higgins, composer Jonathan Dove, repetiteur Gareth Hancock and conductor David Parry during rehearsals.

Director Richard Jones and conductor David Parry (MIKE HOBAN)

LEFT: Helen O'Neill with George Christie on her retirement. She joined Glyndebourne in 1957 as secretary to John Christie, later becoming secretary to Moran Caplat. In the early 1970s she became Head of Press and Public Relations until her retirement in 1996 (MIKE HOBAN)

BELOW: Nicholas Payne, Anthony Whitworth-Jones, Tobias Hoheisel, Nikolaus Lehnhoff, Christof Loy, Nicholas Snowman, David McVicar, John Cox and Peter Horne (Technical Director), summer 1999 (MIKE HOBAN)

BOTTOM: Gus Christie, 1998 (MIKE HOBAN)

OPPOSITE TOP: Visit of the Queen Mother to Glyndebourne, for a performance of *Manon Lescaut*, June 1997 (MIKE HOBAN)

OPPOSITE BOTTOM: Glyndebourne's gardeners, 2004: Kevin Martin, Ron Brockhurst, Stephen Brockhurst, and Head Gardener Chris Hughes. Kevin Martin started working at Glyndebourne in 1994, Ron Brockhurst joined in 1996 and Stephen Brockhurst in 1998. Chris Hughes, Head Gardener from 1988 to 2006, was only the fifth incumbent of the post since the Festival began (MIKE HOBAN)

The audience, 1991 (GÉRARD UFÉRAS)

2000s

... involving, ineluctably, I'm relieved and feel blessed to record, the third generation of the Christie family. My wife and I continued to live at Glyndebourne until the end of 2001, and I continued during these two years to retain a position on the Board of Glyndebourne Productions Ltd and to have an administrative role during the handover period to Gus. It was a handover that thankfully worked seamlessly, causing me to persist with the conceit in these pages of ending the account of each decade with a caesura in mid-sentence to be elided with the opening of the succeeding decade's account.

Each decade of Glyndebourne's development has evolved with the benefit of a 'rear mirror' – like a sentence harking back to the last chapter. I look to my parents' regime with a depth of gratitude for the fundamental principles on which they created Glyndebourne – more than anything, their aim for the highest artistic standards (which they remarkably and indisputably achieved). The sentence left hanging in the air at the end of the last chapter above all needed no full stop.

The 2000 Festival contained the three Mozart/da Ponte operas directed by Vick. The artists who emerged most unscathed from these productions were, in my view, Peter Mattei (Figaro), Mariusz Kwiecien (Count), Barbara Frittoli (Donna Anna), Alessandro Corbelli (Leporello), Louis Langrée, a great Mozartian, conducting *Così*, and of course Andrew Davis conducting *Figaro* and the *Don*.

This happened to be Davis's final year as Glyndebourne's Music Director, a position he had held since 1988 although his association with the company extended back to 1973.

2000

Gus Christie succeeded his father as Chairman

GTO UK premiere of *The Last Supper*

2001

David Pickard joined as General Director

Vladimir Jurowski succeeded Andrew Davis as Music Director

2002

Rodelinda and *Fidelio* performed in Paris

2003

GTO renamed Glyndebourne on Tour

Tristan und Isolde became the first opera by Wagner to be performed at Glyndebourne

2004

He brought penetrating and pervasive intelligence – especially, of course musical intelligence – to his professional work and exploited it often with a beguilingly light touch. He was, I always felt, a perfect fit at Glyndebourne (and I hope he felt the same).

The opening year of the millennium also saw the departure of Snowman as General Director. He was a long-standing friend who exhibited streaks of inspiration – his principal legacy being the appointment of Vladimir Jurowski as Music Director and the engagement of David McVicar to direct *Bohème* for GTO in 2000 and *Carmen* in the 2002 Festival. But his *pièce de résistance* (to date) was Handel's *Giulio Cesare*, which took the public by storm in 2005. But Glyndebourne and Snowman, as it transpired, were sadly not a perfect fit.

In autumn 2000, GTO mounted the production of a work commissioned by Glyndebourne from Birtwistle, *The Last Supper*, which was originally intended to be performed more as an oratorio in consecrated settings. The Deutsche Staatsoper, Berlin, under the music directorship of Daniel Barenboim, however, became involved in the planning process, and Whitworth-Jones agreed to accept the piece as a staged work and as a co-production with the Staatsoper. Martin Duncan, the director, with his designer Alison Chitty did their damnedest to bring dramatic persuasion to the production, and Elgar Howarth, the conductor, was totally in tune with the score.

The following year, David Pickard, at the time the Chief Executive of the Orchestra of the Age of Enlightenment, was persuaded to take up the appointment of General Director at Glyndebourne; and at the same time Jurowski took up the reins as Music Director.

2001 saw the completion of the final piece of the jigsaw in the rebuild, namely the construction of the second rehearsal stage, adjoining the first at the rear of the new development. I was fortunate in persuading the Jerwood Foundation to finance some 40 per cent of the cost – by far the greatest contribution to the rebuild programme. The need for this new facility was occasioned by the ambitions of the outgoing General Director, Snowman, who was bent on increasing the output of new productions – a trend which I notice has continued in more recent years. (Perhaps I shouldn't have provided the physical wherewithal with which to feed this extravagant appetite.) However, the Jerwood Studio, as it is known, is an invaluable adjunct, not just as a rehearsal stage, but as a venue for our education department and for increasing the rollover and development of new vocal talent in the company.

A new production of *Fidelio* (the fourth in Glyndebourne's history) was mounted in 2001, with Rattle conducting and Warner directing. The setting for the dungeon scene was, in my opinion, acoustically the worst I have witnessed on stage at Glyndebourne. Why, oh why, do directors and designers have so little regard for the shape and acoustic properties of their sets so that, as should imperatively be the case, the sound is funnelled and reflected forward to the audience? Furthermore, acoustics and sight lines go hand in hand to the extent that designs should obviously fan out as the stage-set progresses from upstage to downstage. Scarcely a director strays from the centre auditorium to check sight lines during rehearsals at Glyndebourne. I have asked that these imperatives should be highlighted in the design specification given to all directors and designers, but seem to be talking to myself.

The other new production in 2001 was Verdi's *Otello*, directed with unerring intelligence, knowledge and instinct by Hall, in designs by Gunter. Richard Farnes brought idiomatic and dramatic shape to the score. He had been contracted late in the day to replace Valery Gergiev when it was finally and regretfully conceded that his involvement in the production was simply unworkable in his impossibly busy schedule. The clarion, but inflected vocal performance of David Rendall (Verdian tenors of this kind and calibre are rare) in the title role and the profoundly moving performance of Susan Chilcott as Desdemona left a deep imprint on my memory.

2002 saw Gus's full accession. My wife and I moved out of Glyndebourne and Gus and his family moved in. It felt odd

2005

2006

Betrothal in a Monastery had its first professional production in the UK

2007

2008

World premiere of *Love and Other Demons*

2009

Glyndebourne's 75th anniversary

after 67 years for me and 44 years for Mary, but the indulgence of irresponsibility has (at least for me) taken a bit of a grip.

This year saw the first full blast of Snowman's programming legacy with new productions: of Gluck's relatively rarely performed *Iphigénie en Aulide* in a production by Christof Loy and conducted by Bolton; of Weber's musically beautiful but dramatically unwieldy *Euryanthe*, conducted by Elder and directed by Richard Jones, with Anne Schwanewilms memorable in the title role; and thirdly of Bizet's *Carmen*, conducted electrifyingly by Philippe Jordan in a welcome down-to-earth production by McVicar and with Anne Sofie von Otter giving a characteristically intelligent interpretation of the title role.

There were in 2003 four productions new to the Festival, with *Tristan*, as was to be expected, overshadowing them all. It was of course Glyndebourne's first (and, to date, only) foray into the world of Wagner (other than a dotty Organ Room performance of an excerpt from *Die Meistersinger* at the beginning of the 1930s – with my father as Beckmesser!). The conductor, Jiří Bělohlávek, reverting to source material, eliminated the accretions that performing practice over 138 years had brought to all the orchestral parts. The end result often sounded almost like chamber music and the clarity of Wagner's instrumentation was, for me, a revelation. Lehnhoff's production was sure-footed and masterly, fitting perfectly the symbolism of Roland Aeschlimann's dramatically lit single set. The cast, particularly Nina Stemme doing her first Isolde and the incomparable René Pape, ensured a resounding success for Glyndebourne's first leap into Bayreuth's rightful territory.

Idomeneo in a staging by Sellars – using much of the stylisation he had successfully employed in *Theodora* – in designs by Anish Kapoor was a disappointment. Rattle conducted and Magdalena Kožená in the role of Idamante captivated Ilia, the audience and the critics – as well as Rattle, whom she later married (another union 'brokered' by Glyndebourne ...).

The third new production in 2003, *Die Fledermaus*, with Jurowski conducting, was directed by Stephen Lawless in beautiful art-deco designs by Benoît Dugardyn on a revolve. It had all the ingredients for success, but for the presence of a star in the role of Rosalinde. It was beautifully sung by Pamela Armstrong but in the final analysis lacking that unquantifiable elusive quality. Meanwhile Tom Allen shone in the role of Eisenstein – impressively indulgent in the high tessitura.

Bohème in a production very movingly staged by McVicar by GTO in 2000 was new to the Festival in 2003 under Mark Wigglesworth's baton. Rolando Villazón as Rodolfo scored a lot of success in the Company, but was more or less brushed off by the critics. We were all at Glyndebourne totally bemused by this.

2004, Glyndebourne's 70th birthday, saw a resumption of the more traditional pattern of two new productions and four revivals. Snowman's legacy of too many new productions – which were also heavy on vocal and orchestral resources – was in need of re-alignment. New productions were given, firstly of *The Flute*, staged by Adrian Noble under Jurowski's baton, and secondly of a double bill consisting of Rachmaninov's *The Miserly Knight* and Puccini's irresistible comedy, *Gianni Schicchi*, conducted by Jurowski and directed by Annabel Arden. Sergei Leiferkus held centre-stage in the Rachmaninov and Alessandro Corbelli gave a definitive performance in the title role of the Puccini work – supported with lyric ardour by the young lovers, Massimo Giordano as Rinuccio and Sally Matthews as Lauretta.

For me the other highlights of 2004 were firstly Louis Langrée's idiomatically beautiful conducting of *Pelléas et Mélisande*, with Russell Braun and Marie Arnet outstanding in the title roles and Tomlinson repeating his overwhelming performance of Golaud. Secondly, there was Emma Bell's assumption of the title role in *Rodelinda* with total dramatic and vocal authority; and thirdly, Marcus Stenz's stringent but sensitive conducting of *Jenůfa*, with Kathryn Harries taking over the part of the Kostelnička with affecting emotion, a role which until then had been, in harrowing performances, the exclusive property of Anja Silja.

In the following year Rossini's *Cenerentola* (its third production since its 'exhumation' at Glyndebourne in 1952) was conducted by Jurowski and staged by Peter Hall with real insight into the social values which are fundamentally lurking in the plot. It seemed to me that Hall's serious approach and the cast didn't get a consensus of critical approval because the performance lacked Italian/Rossinian flavour ...

But Handel's *Giulio Cesare*, conducted by William Christie, directed by McVicar in collaboration with his movement director, Andrew George, and designed by Robert Jones, had a seismic reaction from the audience and most of the critics. And the cast, particularly Sarah Connolly (Cesare), Danielle de Niese (Cleopatra) and Angelika Kirchschlager (Sesto) was a cup-winner. As our third Handel production in ten years, it seemed to suggest to me that Handel could now be in contention with Mozart (whose operas have been so over-exposed) for pride of place at Glyndebourne.

As a footnote to 2005, mention has to be made of Mackerras's performances of *The Flute* which, in terms of getting effortlessly to the heart of Mozart's music, compared with the best I have heard anywhere.

Così, in a new production directed by Hytner in designs by Vicki Mortimer and conducted by Iván Fischer, was the high point of 2006 – with a quartet of young lovers as good as they get. The other new production, Prokofiev's *Betrothal in a Monastery*, based loosely on Sheridan's *The Duenna*, contained a plot of intricate complexity based on disguise and exchanged identities. Daniel Slater, the director, did his damnedest to unravel the storyline, and Jurowski, who championed the performance of this rarity, made Prokofiev's uneven score almost sound 'even'.

The Independent declared our education department, set up in 1986, 'the most imaginative opera-education department in the country,' for its work in schools and prisons, its work with children with special needs, for its workshops mounted for young people in the towns and cities visited by GTO, for its stagings of community opera, its hip-hop re-interpretation of *Così* and its youth operas (already referred to).

2007 saw new productions of Verdi's *Macbeth* and Bach's oratorio, the *St Matthew Passion*. Jurowski, at that time the LPO's principal conductor designate, was in the process of transforming the spirit and performance of the players in this orchestra. In the case of *Macbeth* the consequences of this were vividly apparent in the pit; and Mark Padmore as the Evangelist in the *Matthew Passion* gave a performance as if sent from Heaven.

A third production new to the Festival was Britten's *The Turn of the Screw* mounted on the 2006 tour. Impeccably directed by Jonathan Kent and ingeniously designed by Paul Brown it scored a huge success compounded by Edward Gardner in the pit. At this time Gardner had recently been appointed Music Director of ENO and so had to relinquish his position as Music Director of our touring company – handing his baton over to an even younger conductor, Robin Ticciati (the present incumbent). These two hugely talented musicians combined with their predecessor, Langrée, make for an impressive line-up of young conductors who have headed Glyndebourne's touring operation in the last ten years.

Finally, in 2008 new productions were mounted of *Poppea* (the third in Glyndebourne's history, albeit in a very different version by Emmanuelle Haïm, the conductor); of Humperdinck's *Hänsel und Gretel*, superlatively conducted by Kazushi Ono and, for me, imaginatively directed by Laurent Pelly; and of a Glyndebourne commission, Peter Eötvös's *Love and Other Demons* based on Gabriel García Márquez's novella. This last piece was conducted with deep involvement by Jurowski which was reflected by an equally committed performance by the LPO and an exceptional cast of singers. Glyndebourne gave its unsparing backing to this production staged by Silviu Purcarete in designs by Helmut Stürmer, which seemed to me to capture the spirit and atmosphere of this literary cocktail containing ingredients represented by ethnic, religious and medical contestants who compete for the salvation of an allegedly rabies-infected girl's soul. The critics in response to this opera, on the whole, sat on the fence. Given the acceptance of a lot of stuff created in the name of extending the operatic repertoire, I felt it deserved better.

I look back over the last 75 years with a sense of pride and gratitude for what my parents created, for the enormous contribution made by all of those who have participated in this journey of endeavour, but above all for the heartbeat which is at the core of Glyndebourne's existence for which I hold my wife, Mary, responsible.

ABOVE: The lake on a winter's morning, 2002 (MIKE HOBAN)

OPPOSITE: The lake during the drought, 2003 (MIKE HOBAN)

Backstage.

BELOW LEFT: Members of the stage technicians moving part of the *Tristan und Isolde* set into place (MIKE HOBAN)

BELOW RIGHT: The coach crash in *La Cenerentola* (MIKE HOBAN)

BOTTOM LEFT: Prompt corner: Stage Manager Stephen Cowin and Assistant Stage Managers, Sophie Leach, Benjamin Lynch and Claire Burslem (MIKE HOBAN)

BOTTOM RIGHT: The Chorus waiting to go on stage in *Betrothal in a Monastery* (MIKE HOBAN)

Making departments.

OPPOSITE PAGE CLOCKWISE FROM TOP LEFT: Clive Ventris (Senior Props Maker) and Michaela Bott (Assistant Props Maker); Boot Store; Christina Margetson, Lorraine Burn and Chloe Prorok in the costume department; Justo Algaba from Spain, a specialist in toreador costumes, during a fitting for *Carmen*; Sacha Chandisingh hand-painting the fabric used to make the Klimt dressing gown worn by von Eisenstein in *Die Fledermaus* (MIKE HOBAN)

GLORIOUS
RED

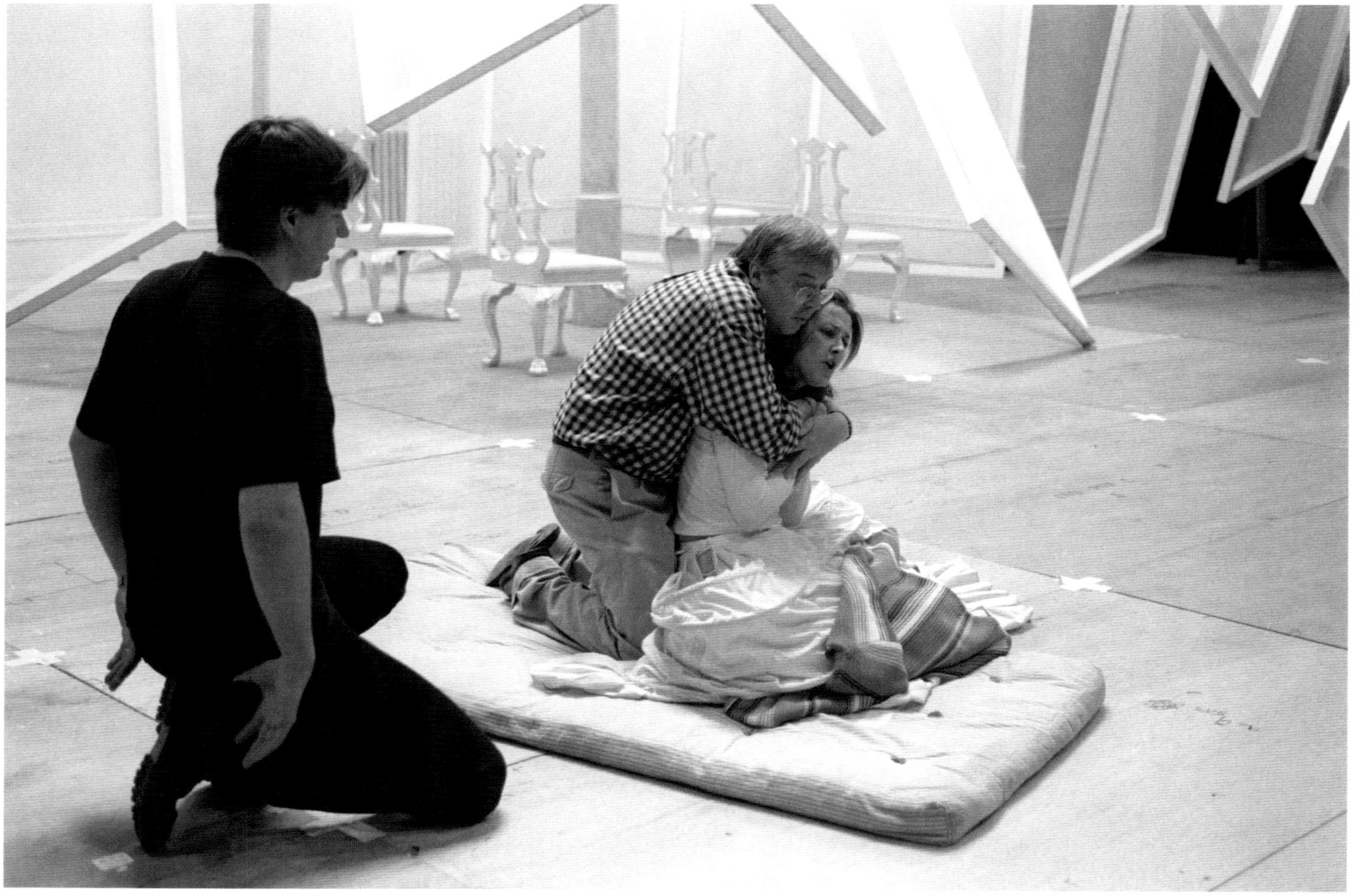

The Mozart/da Ponte productions for 2000, directed by Graham Vick and designed by Richard Hudson.

ABOVE: Graham Vick rehearsing Peter Mattei as Figaro and Christiane Oelze as Susanna in *Le nozze di Figaro* (MIKE HOBAN)

OPPOSITE TOP: Barbara Frittoli and Alessandro Corbelli as Donna Anna and Leporello in *Don Giovanni* (MIKE HOBAN)

OPPOSITE BOTTOM: Barbara Frittoli (MIKE HOBAN)

Rehearsals for *Così fan tutte*, 2000, on part of the *Don Giovanni* set.

TOP: Alan Opie as Don Alfonso, with Paul Austin Kelly (Ferrando) and Nathan Gunn (Guglielmo) (MIKE HOBAN)

OPPOSITE: Alexandra von der Weth (Fiordiligi) and Paul Austin Kelly (Ferrando) (MIKE HOBAN)

Jenůfa, directed by Nikolaus Lehnhoff and designed by Tobias Hoheisel, 2000.

ABOVE: Amanda Roocroft as Jenůfa in rehearsal and in performance (MIKE HOBAN)

OPPOSITE: Anja Silja as the Kostelnička (MIKE HOBAN)

ABOVE: *Otello*, directed by Peter Hall and designed by John Gunter, 2003. Peter Hall in rehearsal with David Rendall (Otello) and Susan Chilcott (Desdemona) (MIKE HOBAN)

OPPOSITE: Rehearsals for *Iphigénie en Aulide*, directed by Christof Loy and designed by Herbert Murauer, 2002 (MIKE HOBAN)
Top left: Gerald Finley as Agamemnon; Top right: Katarina Karnéus as Clitemnestre; Bottom: Veronica Cangemi as Iphigénie (MIKE HOBAN)

TOP: Deborah Warner rehearsing Torsten Kerl and Anja Kampe for her 2006 revival of *Fidelio* (MIKE HOBAN)

ABOVE: Vladimir Jurowski talking to Jonathan Lemalu (Papageno) during rehearsals for *Die Zauberflöte*, watched by director Adrian Noble, 2004 (MIKE HOBAN)

OPPOSITE TOP: Peter Hall, John Bury and George Christie during a fit-up of *A Midsummer Night's Dream* to see if it needed adapting for the new theatre (MIKE HOBAN)

OPPOSITE CENTRE: Simon Rattle with Peter Sellars in the auditorium during *Idomeneo* rehearsals, 2003. Also pictured: Nicholas Kraemer of the OAE, Joe Laurent from the music library and Gareth Hancock of the music staff (MIKE HOBAN)

OPPOSITE BOTTOM: The production desk during rehearsals for *Idomeneo*. Anish Kapoor (designer), Dave Locker (Technical Director), Peter Sellars (director), James F Ingalls (lighting designer), Simon Yapp (AV systems), Robin Carter (lighting) and Keith Benson (Lighting Manager), with Bernard McDonald (Chorus Master) talking to Steven Naylor (Director of Artistic Administration) in the background (MIKE HOBAN)

Rehearsals for *Giulio Cesare*, directed by David McVicar and designed by Robert Jones, 2005.

TOP: Angelika Kirchschlager as Sesto (MIKE HOBAN)

ABOVE: Sarah Connolly as Cesare with director David McVicar (MIKE HOBAN)

OPPOSITE: Danielle de Niese as Cleopatra (MIKE HOBAN)

ABOVE AND LEFT: Education: Opera Experience engaging young children both at home and on tour in Milton Keynes (MIKE HOBAN)

OPPOSITE: Members of the Trinity Boys Choir as the Fairies from *A Midsummer Night's Dream*, playing cricket on the lawn; queuing in the Courtyard Café; and on stage, 2006 (MIKE HOBAN)

Coca-Cola

Glyndebourne Touring Opera, renamed Glyndebourne on Tour in 2003.

ABOVE: Time-lapse image of *The Last Supper* by Harrison Birtwistle which received its UK premiere in autumn 2000 (MIKE HOBAN)

OPPOSITE: Rehearsals for Jonathan Kent's production of Benjamin Britten's *The Turn of the Screw*, which made its first appearance at Glyndebourne in autumn 2006. Top: Kate Royal as the Governess; Far left: Joanna Songi (Flora), Jonathan Kent and Kate Royal; Left: Christopher Sladdin (Miles) and Kate Royal (MIKE HOBAN)

Let me die

PREVIOUS PAGES: Russell Braun and Marie Arnet in the title roles of *Pelléas et Mélisande*, 2004 (MIKE HOBAN)

ABOVE: Mark Padmore as the Evangelist in the *St Matthew Passion*, 2007 (MIKE HOBAN)

OPPOSITE: Robert Gambill and Nina Stemme as Tristan and Isolde, 2003 (MIKE HOBAN)

Pre-performance warm-ups.

ABOVE: Members of the London Philharmonic Orchestra: Santiago Sabino Carvalho (cello), Anthony Byrne (viola) and members of the *Macbeth* on-stage band – Andrew Barclay (co-principal percussion), Jonathan Rees (tuba) and Robin Kennard (bassoon) (MIKE HOBAN)

OPPOSITE: Eleanor Duval, a dancer in *Carmen* warming up backstage (MIKE HOBAN)

Backstage.

ABOVE: *Betrothal in a Monastery*, 2006 (MIKE HOBAN)

OPPOSITE: *Die Zauberflöte*, 2004 (MIKE HOBAN)

ABOVE: Gus Christie as an extra in the Act II finale of *Carmen* (MIKE HOBAN)

LEFT: Gus Christie's twin sons Rom and Jack, as extras in the finale of *Die Zauberflöte* (MIKE HOBAN)

OPPOSITE: Members of the Chorus relaxing in the gardens between rehearsals (MIKE HOBAN)

Company
Members
only

Rehearsal for *Love and Other Demons*, 2008, directed by Silviu Purcarete and designed by Helmut Stürmer.

LEFT: Robert Brubaker as Don Ygnacio and Jean Rigby as Martina Laborde (MIKE HOBAN)

BOTTOM LEFT: Felicity Palmer as Josefa Miranda, Allison Bell as Sierva María and the Glyndebourne Chorus (MIKE HOBAN)

BOTTOM RIGHT: David Pickard, Chorus Master Thomas Blunt and Vladimir Jurowski in discussion on stage during rehearsals. Silviu Purcarete stands to the right (MIKE HOBAN)

OPPOSITE: Backstage preparations (MIKE HOBAN)

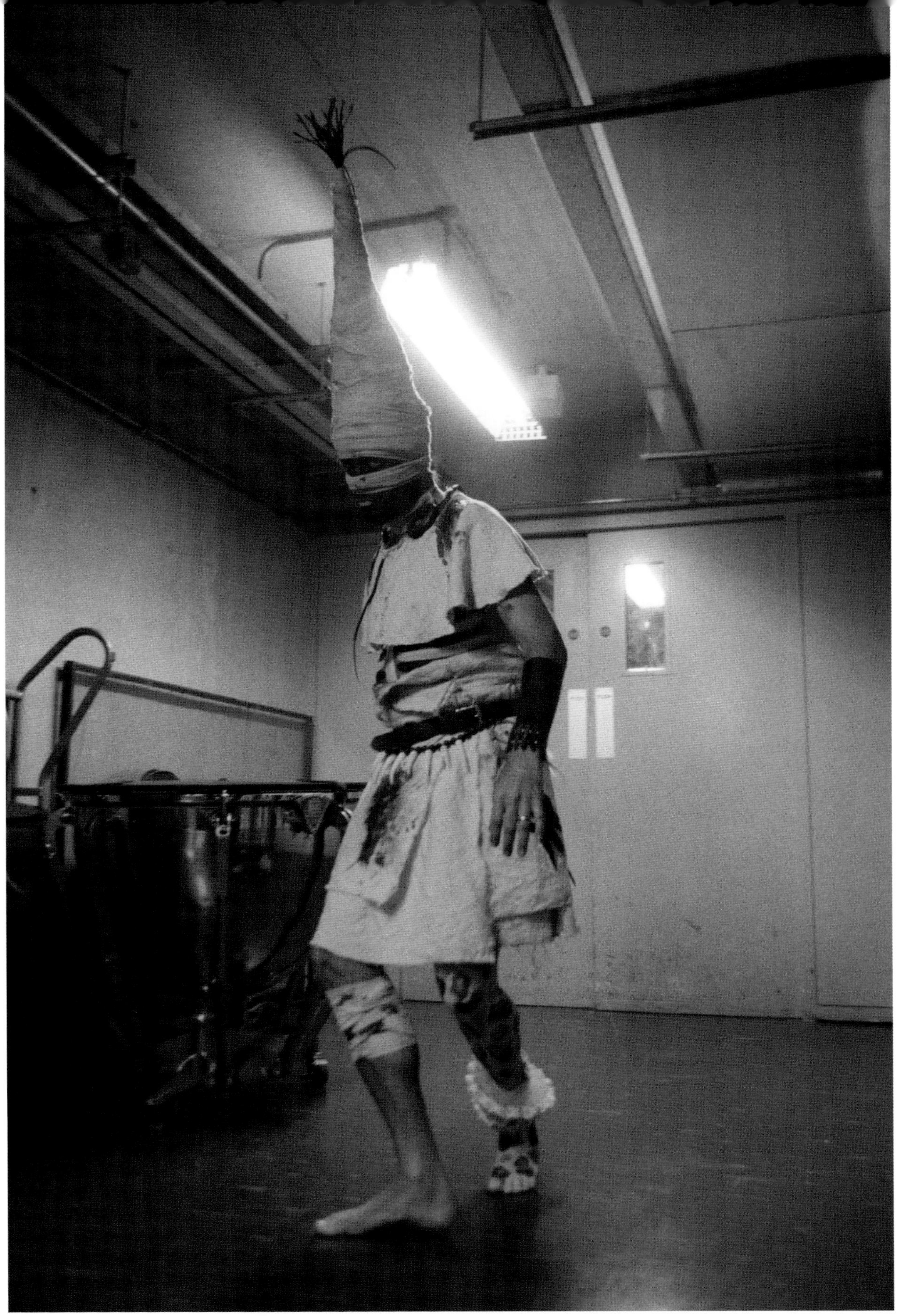

The audience in 2003 (MIKE HOBAN)

PHOTOGRAPHERS AT GLYNDEBOURNE

1934 TO THE PRESENT

VAL WILLIAMS

From its very beginnings in the early 1930s Glyndebourne attracted photographers. Its unique setting, the combination of country-house glamour, a spectacular landscape and its international creative talent were irresistible to photographers and the editors who commissioned them.

As well as professionals, Glyndebourne was documented by amateur photographers, who were often members of staff and the company. With their personal, intimate glimpses behind the scenes, these snapshots add an extra dimension to the collection of professional images.

Although Glyndebourne was regularly visited in the 1930s by press photographers from newspapers and agencies (including *The Daily Herald*, *The Times*, Associated Newspapers and the London News Agency), and also, from time to time, by celebrated portraitists (including Bassano), the most fascinating photographs of its first decade can be found in the work of Ilse Bing and Bill Brandt.

Although paper records from this period were destroyed in the 1960s, and we have no clear evidence why these two talented émigré photographers came to Glyndebourne, it is obvious by the volume of work they produced that they spent considerable periods of time photographing here.

Bill Brandt (1904–1983) photographed Glyndebourne in 1936, the same year that his iconic book *The English at Home* was published, establishing him as one of the great photo-documentarists of the inter-war years. German-born Brandt had arrived in London from Europe in 1934, but his career as a photojournalist did not begin until he started to work for *Lilliput* magazine in 1937. It is therefore unlikely (though not impossible) that Brandt was commissioned to document Glyndebourne. He may well have been directed there by the extensive network of émigré and English contacts who helped him locate subjects for *The English at Home*.

After his visit(s) to Glyndebourne in 1936 Brandt produced an album of 92 mounted photographs, which was either presented to or purchased by the Christie family. The album is a carefully sequenced and structured day-in-the-life record, with Brandt using a visual methodology he would later employ in his extensive photojournalism of the 1940s. Brandt enjoyed making albums (some can be seen in the collection at the V&A), but these personal albums were highly varied in picture size and subject matter. The Glyndebourne album is altogether plainer in concept, but the photographs it contains show Brandt's fascination with gardens, the rural landscape and the English upper classes, all of which would feature in his work for years to come. Brandt's documentation of house and garden, theatre interiors and exteriors, the wardrobe and technical departments, singers, conductors and chorus, rehearsals, performances, audiences and al fresco dining, forms a unique window onto a remarkable history.

Photographer Ilse Bing made her only known visit to the UK when she was commissioned to photograph at Glyndebourne in 1937. Born in Frankfurt in 1899, she lived and worked as a successful photographer in Paris from 1930 to 1941, when she emigrated to the US. Working exclusively with a Leica camera, Bing had close relationships with a number of magazines and newspapers, including *Das Illustriete Blat*, *L'Illustration*, *Le Monde*, *Illustre* and *Regards*. She also worked for *Vogue* and *Harpers Bazaar*. Any one of these publications could have commissioned Bing to photograph the fledgling English opera house. Although the Glyndebourne Archive has extensive records of individual syndicated photographs taken of Glyndebourne by Bing, which were published in newspapers across Europe, the original commissioner is not known.

In Paris Bing moved in artistic and musical circles – her marriage to pianist and teacher Konrad Wolff in the early 1930s was an important connection with the music world.

Correspondence between Rudolf Bing (no relation to Ilse) and Audrey Mildmay (Mrs John Christie) shows how eager Glyndebourne's founders were to obtain photographic records of performances. In his letter of January 1938, Rudolf Bing assures Mrs Christie that he would 'ask her [Ilse Bing] to lunch tomorrow and to show me all her photographs ... it may be advisable to buy some – in particular scene photos – but I shall, of course, let you and John see and know first what I suggest'.

Whether or not as a result of this meeting, Glyndebourne did acquire a set of Bing photographs, many of which were loose prints, but there is also an album of 25 black-and-white photographs. Each image is signed 'Ilse Bing, Paris' on the front. Among the productions photographed were *Le nozze di Figaro* and *Così fan tutte*. The album includes pictures of the house and the theatre exterior and meadow, but most are of productions.

In 1940, Bing and Wolff were interned in France until they were able to sail for the US. Although Bing's photographs survived the war in Paris, many of them, including all the English images, were destroyed on arrival in the US, making the photographs which survive in the Glyndebourne Archive doubly precious.

The 1940s inevitably brought change to Glyndebourne as Europe descended into war. The last pre-war production organised by the opera house was the 1940 national tour of *The Beggar's Opera*. The photographer commissioned to document the production was the young Angus McBean (1904–1990), who in the late 1940s would revolutionise the way in which performances were photographed. Until the early 1940s, theatre photography had been very much a sideline for professional photographers and those used by Glyndebourne in its early years. It was notoriously difficult to capture the energy and vividness of performance as photographers depended on theatre lighting to illuminate the scene rather than on the string of directional lights used by studio photographers.

McBean already had a powerful affinity with theatre when he began his photographic career. He was a self-taught mask maker and had formed a close friendship with the Motleys, Sophia, Margaret and Elizabeth Harris, who designed the costumes for *The Beggar's Opera*, produced by John Gielgud, who also later became one of McBean's favourite sitters. McBean's talent had been noticed by the society photographer Hugh Cecil. Working as Cecil's assistant, McBean learned important techniques of studio lighting and portraiture. Commissioned by Ivor Novello in 1936 to photograph *The Happy Hypocrite*, McBean's career as a theatre photographer had begun.

Though McBean's theatre photographs from the 1940s, 1950s and 1960s may look over-stylised and stilted to contemporary eyes, the innovations he made, including full photography rehearsals with photo lighting and the power to direct performers specifically for photographs, were of huge significance, as was his understanding, as a mask and props maker, of the physicality of stage presence. In the post-war period, when Glyndebourne re-opened, McBean's work was held in such high esteem that he was able to insist on a full-cast weekend photo call for Benjamin Britten's

The Rape of Lucretia. Glyndebourne's General Manager, Rudolf Bing, thought McBean's photographs 'excellent' and wrote to him in January 1940 to order 23 photographs of *The Beggar's Opera*, 'for exhibition at the Theatres and for press purposes'. McBean charged two shillings and sixpence for each print, which included the copyright. He also sold photographs to individual performers, including a set of six postcards and two 12x10-inch prints to singer Linda Grey in May, 1940.

Although McBean's great rival, theatre photographer John Vickers, produced work for Glyndebourne when he photographed the Children's Theatre in 1947, McBean was clearly Glyndebourne's favoured photographer.

Glyndebourne Opera closed during the war years, and became a temporary home for evacuee infants. Many fascinating photographs from this period survive, most significantly snapshots taken by women who worked in the nurseries. The transformation of Glyndebourne from elegant country house and gardens to nursery and vegetable plot is a remarkable part in its history, preserved through photography.

Technical advances in photography and in ways of thinking about the medium affected the documentation of Glyndebourne in significant ways. McBean had changed the way that performance looked in photographs, and photojournalists, who had been accustomed to portraying the chaos of war, were now commissioned to document a cultural scene that was becoming increasingly important in the everyday life of British people. The Magnum photojournalist and *Life* photographer George Rodger, who photographed the liberation of Belsen in 1945, travelled down to East Sussex in July 1946 (along with Gerti Deutsch and Angus McBean) to photograph Benjamin Britten's new opera, *The Rape of Lucretia*. He was clearly struck, as Brandt had been before him, by the country-house style of outdoor picnics and evening dress. Rodger's 1940s photograph of opera-goers enjoying a picnic in the car park became emblematic of the way Glyndebourne would be interpreted by documentary photographers in the decades to come.

The 1950s saw a number of distinguished photographers visiting Glyndebourne. The young documentary photographer Jane Bown (b.1925) visited Glyndebourne for the first time in 1955. Commissioned by *The Observer*, Bown made an elegiac series of photographs of the audience in the gardens. Like Rodger and Brandt, she too was fascinated by the glamour and opulence of Glyndebourne, seen through the prism of a Britain still mired in post-war austerity. Fascinated too by the social complexities of Glyndebourne were the Magnum photographers Cornell Capa and Henri Cartier Bresson, who, along with the documentarist Erich Auerbach, all photographed opera-goers during the 1950s.

By the 1960s, Angus McBean had been supplanted as Glyndebourne's principal photographer by Lewes photographer Guy Gravett. By this time McBean was no longer such a powerful force in theatre photography; his style fell from favour as theatre managers, ever eager to attract new audiences, leaned towards more 'natural' images.

Originally invited to take portraits of George and Rosamond Christie in the Organ Room in 1945, Gravett went on to photograph *Le nozze di Figaro* at Glyndebourne in 1951, and by the mid 1950s his connection with Glyndebourne became more formal. Though Gravett's production photographs also have an inevitable formality, he made serious efforts to modernise the way that opera was presented through photographs. Gravett was an all-rounder, able to adapt himself as well to photographing productions as to capturing informal shots in the gardens and during rehearsals.

At a moment when its influence was waning, Glyndebourne could not depend on the whims of editors and star photographers to produce the photographs it needed. Gravett had both the organisational qualities and the artistic vision necessary to produce both workmanlike stage shots and an ongoing documentation of the social dimensions of Glyndebourne. The relationship between Gravett and Glyndebourne proved to be a strong and long-lasting one. He documented its resurgence in the 1970s, and it is because of his photography (plus that of visiting photographers Zoë Dominic and dance photographer Anthony Crickmay) that we have such an enduring record of the years when David Hockney, Jonathan Miller, Peter Hall, John Bury and John Cox changed the face of opera, bringing a startling theatrical modernity to what had been seen by many as far removed from the new radical culture of the 1970s.

For aspiring photojournalists of that decade, the photographs taken by Tony Ray Jones (1941–1972) at Glyndebourne in 1967, some of which were used in his seminal book *A Day Off* (published posthumously in 1974), were an inspiration. Ray Jones was a passionate defender of documentary photography, and a stern critic of those who practised it. Energetic, abrasive and hugely knowledgeable about photography's emerging stars (including Gary Winogrand and Diane Arbus), he also possessed a remarkable sense of heritage. Although his views on photography were entirely modern and challenged the status quo, his interest in British society, with its anachronisms and its surreal qualities, was the driving force of the work he produced before his untimely death in 1972. Ray Jones was fascinated by 'Englishness', whether it was expressed through the amateur actors of the York Mystery Plays, working people at the seaside or Glyndebourne opera-goers. Undoubtedly influenced by Bill Brandt's magical 1930s collection *The English at Home*, Ray Jones brought a lightness of touch and a particular sense of irony to documentary photography that was never more present than in his photographs of Glyndebourne.

Though photographers continued to visit Glyndebourne during the 1980s, the work of Guy Gravett dominates the period. By the mid 1980s, a new group of British documentarists were revelling in the social complexities thrown up during the heady years of the Thatcher government. While Ray Jones had glimpsed an enduring 'Englishness' in Glyndebourne's gardens, picnics and evening-dressed patrons, younger photographers such as Martin Parr, Paul Graham and Anna Fox were more interested in creating an oblique critique of social conditions in the Thatcher years. Glyndebourne was decorous, elegant and socially fascinating, but the shopping malls, retail parks, faux heritage sites and unemployment offices of the 1980s promised richer rewards to photographers committed to producing a portrayal of Britain at its brashest.

Aware of contemporary photographers' desire to produce a social critique, plus feeling increasingly protective of its privacy (which coincided with the rise of the paparazzi in the 1980s), Glyndebourne became wary of photographers, as it had not been in previous years. Glyndebourne, with its code of evening dress and its long dinner interval, could easily have been pictured as elitist, out of step with contemporary mores and social concerns, regardless of the fact that many of its patrons are dyed–in-the wool opera fans rather than aspiring socialites. Guy Gravett's quiet chronicle of the patterns of people, places and performance continues to be our major source of information about Glyndebourne through the 1980s and early 1990s.

By the mid 1990s, photographer Mike Hoban began to undertake the vast task of documenting Glyndebourne. In what is probably the most comprehensive and varied picture of the organisation in all its many facets, Hoban has produced a chronicle of Glyndebourne with enormous dedication and energy. From picnickers in the gardens, to backstage, the mystical landscape which surrounds the theatre, and in particular, the rehearsals and productions staged by the opera house over the last 15 years, Hoban's is a complex and absorbing documentary. Unlike those photographers who have preceded him, he is confronted by a vast array of technical methodologies, ranging from large format to high-speed digital photography (though he admits to preferring a Leica (35mm camera) and black-and-white film), and these are employed throughout his work to produce a many-sided portrait. Photography of performance, as McBean, Gravett and others knew, is a formidably difficult task – never more so than when confronting the high stylisation of opera. Hoban has approached the mighty spectacle with both the austere sensibility of the documentarist and the stylistic mindset of the theatre photographer, always trying to preserve an intimacy elusive on Glyndebourne's extensive stage sets.

For Glyndebourne, photography has been a central part of its dramatic and engaging story, bearing witness to change, to personality, to passion and sometimes to failure. The photographs in this book represent only a fraction of the archive's collection, but demonstrate what an alluring subject Glyndebourne has been to a wide range of photographers, from Britain and abroad. Its tantalising 'Englishness', mixed with productions of high international status, its star performers, its gardeners, stage technicians, costumes, picnics, green room, studios, gardens, workshops and its proud sense of its own remarkable history have presented myriad opportunities to a beguiling succession of photographers.

INDEX OF OPERAS

The Editors would like to express their thanks to Joanna Townsend and Julia Aries for their invaluable assistance and support, and all the staff at Glyndebourne who helped in the production of this book; to all the photographers and copyright holders, in particular Helen O'Neill who was, in large measure, responsible for the setting up of the Archive, and also to Mike Hoban for the supply and preparation of Guy Gravett's photographs.
We express our thanks also to the University of the Arts London.

All the photographs that appear in this book form part of the Glyndebourne Archive.

Glyndebourne
Lewes
East Sussex
BN8 5UU

First published in 2009

A catalogue record of this book is available from the British Library

ISBN: 978-1-84724-865-7

Printed and bound in China ***

Editorial, layout and production Quercus Publishing, London

Designed by seagulls.net

10 9 8 7 6 5 4 3 2 1

PICTURE ACKNOWLEDGEMENTS
© The Ilse Bing Estate/Courtesy Edwynn Houk Gallery, New York: pages 10-11, 31, 32
A Console: pages 12-13, 16
© Bill Brandt/Bill Brandt Archive Ltd: pages 13(t), 14(t), 18-19, 22(t), 27, 33(t), 39, 42, 45
The Times/NI Syndication: pages 20, 55, 84(t)
Daily Herald Archive at the NMeM/Science & Society Picture Library: pages 21, 22(b), 26(t), 29, 38, 40
Felix Man/Hulton Archive/Getty Images: page 26(b)
Cecil Kerr: page 30
Sussex Express: pages 28(b), 104
Bassano Studios/Glyndebourne Estate: pages 34-5
Angus McBean: pages 50-1, 62(b), 64-5, 67-9, 91, 92(b), 99
The John Vickers Theatre Collection: page 56
Erich Auerbach: pages 58(t), 62(t), 108
Photographs by Keystone–France, Camera Press London: pages 59(t), 60, 61(t)
George Rodger/Time & Life Pictures/Getty Images: pages 63(b), 72–3
Malcolm Dunbar: page 66
© Vogue/The Condé Nast Publications Ltd: page 71
BBC Photo Library: pages 78, 82-3
Guy Gravett: pages 76, 79, 87-90, 92(t), 94-8, 100-1, 102(b), 114-16, 118-24, 126-46, 150-1, 156(t), 157-8, 159(t), 160-3, 167, 168(t), 169-171, 173-4, 176-9, 184, 188-202(t), 203, 212-13
Cornell Capa/Time & Life Pictures/Getty Images: pages 80-1, 103, 105, 109
Herb Greer: page 81
Edward Reeves, Lewes: pages 84(b), 221
The Queen photographs courtesy of The National Magazine Company: pages 75, 85, 107-8
Roger Wood Photographic Collection at Royal Opera House Collections: pages 77, 86, 102(t), 106
Photographs by Snowdon, Camera Press, London: page 93, 107
Henri Cartier-Bresson/Magnum: page 110
Jane Bown/The Guardian News & Media: pages 111, 204-5
British Insulated Callender's Cables Ltd: page 117
The Scotsman Publications Ltd: page 125
National Media Museum/Science & Society Picture Library: page 147
© Zoë Dominic: pages 152-3, 164-6, 168(b), 180-1, 202(b)
Photographer Anthony Crickmay, ©V&A Images, Victoria and Albert Museum: pages 154-5
Donald Cooper: pages 156(b), 172
Chris Cormack: page 159(c&b)
Philip Ingram: page 175
Estate of Anthony Kersting: pages 186-7
© Sussex Police: page 210
Harrier Productions/David Bowie Photography: page 211
Joel Hopkins: pages 214, 217
© Crown copyright/NMR: page 215
Gus Christie: pages 216(l), 218(t), 219
Richard Davies: pages 216(r), 218(c&b), 220, 237(t)
© Mike Hoban 1994-2008: pages 222-236(t), 237-41, 247-81
© Gérard Uféras 1991: pages 242-3